D0924209

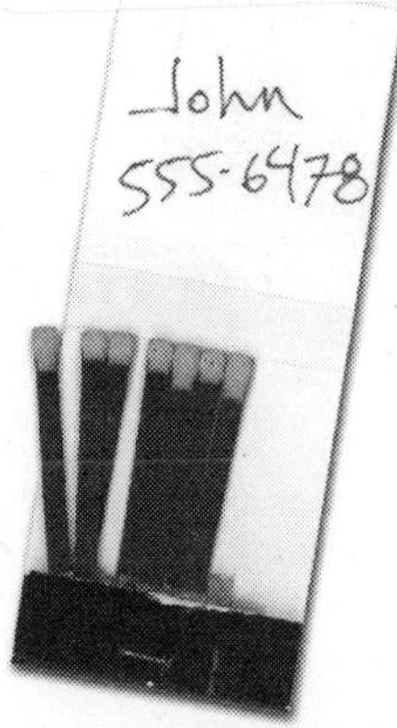
John
555-6478

PLAYING with MATCHES

misadventures in dating

Anchor Canada

LIBRARY AND ARCHIVES CANADA CATALOGUING IN PUBLICATION

Cameron, Amy

Playing with matches : misadventures in dating / Amy Cameron.

ISBN 0-385-66107-X

1. Dating (Social customs)—Humor. 2. Man-woman relationships—Humor. I. Title.

PN6231.D3C34 2005 818'.607 C2004-906608-0

Cover image: Sasha / Getty Images
Cover and text design: Kelly Hill
Printed and bound in Canada

Published in Canada by
Anchor Canada, a division of
Random House of Canada Limited

Visit Random House of Canada Limited's website: www.randomhouse.ca

TRANS 10 9 8 7 6 5 4 3 2 1

Dedicated to the memory of my darling grandmother

— Eleanor Roblin Bone Dahl —

whose advice on finding the perfect partner amounted to "someone who's funny, honest, and has a great ass."

Contents

Having the habit therefore of knowing her men friends well, a young girl is not going to imagine a stranger, no matter how perfect he may appear to be, anything but an ordinary human man after all. And in finding out his bad points as well as his good, she is aided and abetted, encouraged or held in check, by the members of the group to which she belongs.

EMILY POST, *Etiquette*, 1922

Introduction

SUNDAY AFTERNOON. Four of us—the single women at the baby shower—are hunched in a corner drinking Bloody Marys and ignoring a chorus of cooing over a Winnie the Pooh breast-feeding pillow. "All night long he talked to me through the bloody cat," Julie complains. "'Does Mummy like to snuggle? Isn't Mummy funny?'" I snort my drink all over her winter-white skirt. She brushes it off without thinking and continues: "I bought leather knee-high boots for this guy?"

Every woman who has ever stumbled through an awkward evening with Mr. Very Wrong shares the common language of humiliation. Nothing is as humbling as trying to present yourself in the best light (candlelight, to be sure) only to have the evening go wildly off course. At some point during the date, the fluorescent lighting of mismatched pheromones switches on and you're willing to give up the whispery hope of your first child to be home in bed with a bowl of popcorn. After all the preparations—picking a new outfit, shaving legs, straightening hair, applying a fresh coat of Viva Glam, and scanning *The Globe* for a quick fix of potential topics of conversation—a date gone wrong is frustrating. Not only a waste of time, it's almost always embarrassing.

The market is saturated with books on How to Find a Man. There's plenty of confusing advice out there on the do's and don'ts of dating. Everyone hears the success stories. Everyone knows the recipe for an ideal date: one nice guy plus a great-hair day, a cup of good lighting, remove five pounds, a sprinkle of new perfume, and a liberal splash of Stoli vodka. That someone actually manages to cook up a date like this is rare.

DO	DON'T
Keep the conversation going	Babble on too long
Ask him about himself	Pry
Be open	Talk about exes
Wear makeup	Look like a whore

Playing with Matches is for women who, let's face it, have much more experience with recipes for disaster than recipes for romance. We know that there are more bad dates out there than good ones. Intellectually, we also know that these misadventures build character. As Mom says, what doesn't kill you makes you stronger, right?

The act of hanging out with someone to see if sparks fly is an integral part of learning who we are and what we like. A test run with different types of people teaches us to communicate and explore our own personal love limits. Can I cuddle with a man who blows his nose in a cloth napkin? Do I like to spank my lover? Do I have something in common with the director of a funeral home? Does a pierced nipple bother me? How about a pierced scrotum?

Women know about the X factor. No matter how carefully you pick your dates, plan the location, choose the menu, and pack your purse, the X factor can throw everything off balance in an instant. It can be anything: a tipsy grandmother, an impertinent dog, even a deep-seated fear of chocolate.

With our friends, we rejoice in the dates that provide such entertainment—embrace our misadventures, share the pain, and find the humour. We need something to remind us that no matter how awful our dates were, there's always someone else with a worse story. In the winter of 2004, I hosted a number of Bad Date Dinners, inviting small groups of close friends and acquaintances to share gruesome dating details over comfort food. At the end of every evening, people walked away with new friendships and cheeks stained with tears of laughter.

An initial e-mail request for tragic dating stories garnered well over two hundred replies. Women from around the world contributed their hilarious tales to this book. For close to a year, stories from Ireland, England, Asia, the United States, Australia, Germany, France, and, of course, Canada popped up in my inbox. Women in bars, overhearing conversations about this book, piped up with their stories. At my gym, where I'd placed a call for bad dates, a woman accosted me on the weight machine with a terrific story about sleeping with her sister's boyfriend, who also happened to be *her* boyfriend's roommate.

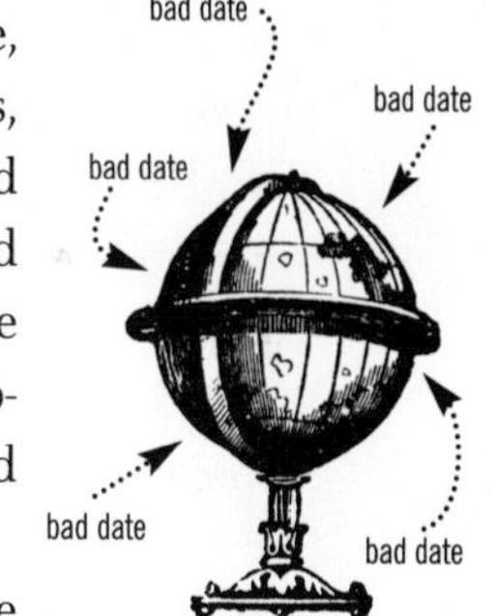

There are bad dates from every decade between 1950 and 2004. Some are outrageous. Others will seem innocent to our postmodern ears. But these are the dates that women from all ages and all countries *chose* to send in. It's what they remember, dozens of years and dates later, as being a "bad date." These stories are ones that women have carried with them, tucked deep in a pocket of their emotional purse.

One woman, for example, wrote of a trip she took in the early 1950s. Twenty-one years old and single, she started her trip in Wolfsburg, Germany, where she was asked on a date by a young German man. They went for a drive, ending up at a lookout over the city. "As we sat looking out at the lights," she wrote to me, "Albrecht's long right arm slipped in behind me and he began making moves. The cars had only bench seats at that time, so he moved over to be close to me. I was horrified when I realized what his intentions were, so I pretended to be fascinated with the car and began asking questions about what the various lights were on the dash. Really stupid questions!" She ducked out of the passenger-side door and moved around to the driver's seat. After this dance continued for a while, Albrecht got the hint and took her home. Fifty years later, she writes, "It's a date I don't like remembering."

Some of the dates are painful. Most are very funny. All are real. The generosity of the women and men who contributed to this book stuns me, and I will be forever grateful. To those people, thank you. You shared all the nasty and delicious details, were beyond patient with me, and, as a result, turned tragedy into comedy. To keep up my end of the bargain, names and details were changed not only to encourage all the juicy tidbits but also to protect the not so innocent.

Many of the pseudonyms were picked by the contributors. One woman, saddled with an old-fashioned name, always dreamt of being called "Meadow." Another chose her late grandmother's name because, as she explained, "I think it's been a while since she rolled over in her grave." Others were chosen to reflect a characteristic in the woman whose story I am sharing. The rest were pulled from baby name Web sites.

Before we go any further, I must add that any embellishments are my own. And any similarity to *another* person, living or dead, is purely coincidental.

As a newspaper and magazine journalist, I've heard some bizarre stories. But nothing compares to what comes out during an evening with girlfriends and a few bottles of wine. My friends and I learned early on to laugh at ourselves in love. We collect anecdotes—I've even been known to write down details I want to remember while my date is in the bathroom.

Like so many women, and as a survivor of countless terrible evenings, I consider myself an expert. I've dated an overweight manic eater who picked fights, and an anaesthetist who really did put me to sleep. I've gone out with a man who carved my name into his arm, and a man who tattooed his own name on his bicep in case he ever forgot it. Every new bad date made me swear off men forever. Until, of course, I was asked out again. Today, my good *bad* stories are legend among friends and family. "Don't worry," people say as they listen to someone else's recent misadventure, "at least he didn't carve your name into his arm."

Bad dates happen. Every night, another woman returns home reeling from a missed match. Finally, these women will be able to seek succour in the humour of shared experiences when there's no one to call at 2 a.m. *Playing with Matches* will make you laugh, cry, and thank the dating goddesses that at least it didn't happen to you.

Monday 1983

11 DAY Boxing Day DATE December 26

Tottie, do ever feel the need of romance? I do! I've never kissed a boy! I'm in Gr. 6 now and I don't feel I'm ready for too much romance but I have none! Mike likes me and thats good but He's to short and not "MATURE" enough for me. in black book

12:10 AM DAY Tuesday DATE 84-02-14

Tottie, I'm sorry I haven't written to you but that last entry is wrong!! I have kissed a boy!!!!!!!!!!!! etc...

Mike, too! But, only on the cheek! You see, I have to tell someone! So, here goes! By the way, it's Valentine's day

cont... in black book

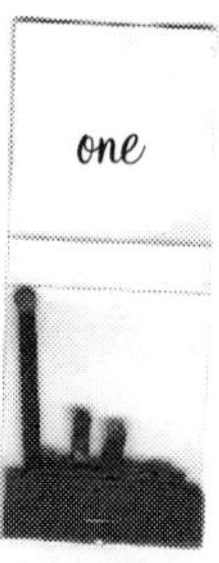

The First Date

MURRAY IS A GOD. A curly haired, blond Adonis with washboard abs and piercing blue eyes. After a summer spent on his father's boat, he's tan, svelte, and has an easy swagger that belies his thirteen years.

I'm twelve and I love Murray with every fibre of my gawky frame. I've loved him for a lifetime—six long, miserable, heart-aching months. At night, I walk my dog past his house, shooing her into his yard so I can peer in the windows. I've befriended his little sister. Using bright red embroidery thread, I sew his name on my underpants. Murray. I want nothing more than for him to be my first kiss. Murray. I'll die happy if only his bee-stung lips touch mine. (I'll die moderately happy if we just hold hands.)

It's a steamy afternoon in late August when Murray calls. He asks me to a barbecue at his friend Tom's house. My mind becomes instant mush, I mumble "Sure-yeah," and we arrange for him to pick me up (swoon) on his bike. We'll ride to Tom's together.

I've dreamt about our first date. Murray leads me into a green, mossy dell, sunlight filtering through the leaves. He pulls me down to sit amid the violets. I can smell his musky boy scent. "I always had a crush on you," he says, a blush forming on his cheeks. He offers me his school tie or, better yet, his school ring, as a token of his adoration. We hold hands. He kisses me. It's like a butterfly landing on my lips.

I pay no attention to the fact that there isn't a dell anywhere near my neighbourhood. I've never seen Murray blush, and his school probably doesn't even do the ring thing. I don't care. I'm caught up in romance.

On the appointed day, at the appointed hour, the doorbell rings. I'm in my sister's room, willing my bladder to hold fast. I've imagined every scenario and done everything to prepare. My armpits, for the first time ever, are shaved (I staunched the blood with Kleenex). I used my strawberry lolly lip gloss and squeezed six blackheads. I let my sister dress me in her clothes and I'm ready.

And now he's here. Downstairs.

"Keep him waiting, Amy," my sister counsels. "It'll make him want you more." At fourteen, she's older and wiser. So I sit still and listen as my grandmother greets him at the door.

"Amy," she bellows, "your little friend Murray is here and he *is* as cute as you said he was."

Three things happen: tears spring to my eyes, my sister starts laughing, and Murray says, "I'll wait outside." I stumble downstairs.

"Have fun, dear," says my (disowned) grandmother as I walk to my bike. Murray is already pedalling by the time I swing a leg over the seat. My grandmother, a gin and tonic in hand, toddles out to the front yard to wave goodbye. I set off. *I can salvage this,* I whisper to myself. *It's okay. We're one house away and free,* I think, when my grandmother's voice shatters the summer evening.

"And remember, darling, keep your legs crossed."

Murray's bike swerves, narrowly missing a parked car. Tears stream down my cheeks. We don't speak all night.

Three months later, Tom is my first kiss.

❋

THINK OF A BOX. It can be any size. It's wrapped in heavy, cream-coloured linen paper, the kind used for posh letterhead and wedding invitations. Around this box is a lovely pink ribbon—not that cheap kind you buy at the drugstore but a soft, wide Swiss satin ribbon that ties a perfect bow and requires nothing but length to make it curl.

This box is waiting for you on your bed. There isn't a card. Before pulling the ribbon from its knot, you pause to savour the possibilities. Is it two first-class tickets to Florence? A pair of coveted Manolo Blahnik *peau de soie* slingbacks? Platinum, fur-lined handcuffs? A (gasp) ring?

You can't help but indulge in the fantasy.

This, my friends, is the first date.

Anything can happen.

Sure. Say what you want. We're cynical, jaded, distrustful, and world weary. We're experts at the dating game, and we hate it. We live in perpetual disappointment. The first date is a necessary evil.

We say these things because all first dates are based on dreams. Imbedded deep within our hardened hearts is a seed of hope that on this first date, you will meet The One. Even The One for Right Now. With the right person,

He who climbs a ladder
must begin at the first step.
Lucky Numbers 2, 4, 31, 34, 36, 39

you might end up married in Las Vegas or dancing naked at Mardi Gras. We've all heard stories of a first date that "lasted thirty-five years and counting." Even as we roll our eyes, we secretly hope to say the same some day.

This is why, when we open that gorgeous, promising box sitting on our bed to discover a grungy, sweat-stained baseball cap, we're sad and just a little angry. Witnessing the destruction of our fantasies is never fun.

So, linger a little longer over the wrapped gift. Dream. More often, it's better than seeing what's inside. That's why first dates are addictive. The potential. The antici . . . pation.

❄

SARAH IS READY AT SEVEN.

She's excited about this date. She's been eyeing Jerry for months. An emergency room nurse at a hospital on the east coast, Sarah has a soft spot for EMTs (Emergency Medical Technicians, a.k.a. Ambulance Guys). Generally, she doesn't date people from work, but Jerry's brought her coffee a couple of times and massaged her shoulders once. He has warm hands and, in their business, that counts for a lot. He has dark curly hair that falls into his eyes and he shares her morbid hospital humour.

They live in a town not known for its beauty but as a solid, steady place that tries to keep up with the world. It holds just over sixty thousand people and Sarah is certain she's dated, and rejected, most of them. This is why she agrees to go on a date with Jerry. The pool of available men is getting ever smaller.

On D-Day, Sarah prepares carefully. She gets a haircut and has her nails done in a French manicure. She buys a funky red top from the Gap and pulls on her tight, hot tamale jeans.

Jerry picks her up at eight. "I thought we'd grab a drink," he says.

"Sounds good," she replies.

Jerry drives across town and pulls into Tim's.

Tim Hortons.

The doughnut shop.

Pulling up to the drive-through window, Jerry orders two Cokes. "I thought we'd go back to my place." he says. "That okay?"

Sarah is speechless.

Seven minutes later, Jerry leads her into a basement apartment that smells like dirty laundry and ancient cat piss. "Here," he says, dumping her coat on the floor with one hand and grabbing a bottle with the other. "Some rum, Madame?" He lifts the clear plastic top of her Tim Hortons cup and pours in a hefty shot. "I rented a movie for us," Jerry says, doctoring his own Coke.

Sarah sits. She sips her drink through the straw.

Jerry turns on the TV and flicks off the light. He presses play. The film has already been forwarded through the credits, and an image immediately comes to life. Two women. Naked.

Sarah chokes on her Tim Hortons Cuba Libre. Onscreen, one woman crouches over a man, giving him a blow job, while the other woman sits on his face. Just as Sarah opens her mouth to protest, the movie cuts to a close-up of the man's penis. Semen spurts through the air and lands with a wet splat on the woman's face. "I love that part," sighs Jerry.

Sarah is home by nine.

❋

FEBRUARY 1, 9:43 P.M.

Ellen's had days not worth living. Not that she means to be alarmist. She doesn't want to jump off a building or drop the toaster in the tub. She just doesn't believe that she should have had to live through certain days. She's grown enough as a person, thank you very much.

Some of Ellen's days are fantastic. Everything is in sync: traffic lights, hair, a project at work. That's what is *supposed* to happen, but today was a not-worth-living day. Really, she should've battened down the hatches and hid: holed up with a bag of Doritos and a pack of smokes and kept the lights off.

Tonight was the date with Will. Ellen and Will met two weeks ago at Cindy's party and chatted. Will is delicious. Rippling, vibrant, hard. They didn't talk for long, but when Ellen walked away from him, her knees were jelly.

In fact, Ellen even experienced minor chest pain the next morning when Cindy called to ask if she could give Will her number. He wanted her number. Ellen's number. Lord help her, she was on fire.

The phone rang two days later. "Hello, Ellen," he said, voice rumbling across the line. They talked for half an hour—work, play, family, the usual. Needn't have bothered since, as the saying goes, he had her at hello. Will, oblivious to all of the shaking and sweating going on at the other end of the line, asked if he could call her again.

And he did, this time to invite Ellen to meet him after work tonight. A waiter at a sleek, chic restaurant with hors d'oeuvres that cost more than her perfume, Will wanted to have a quick drink there before moving on to another bar that had just opened around the corner.

If Ellen were honest, she would admit that Will is the best looking man to ever ask her out. She couldn't believe her luck. So she went the extra mile. She waxed everything worth waxing. She contemplated a Brazilian wax just in case, but after full legs, pits, upper lip, and regular bikini line, she was sobbing from the pain.

She scrubbed her apartment, hid her tampons and soap for acne-prone skin. She wore her only matching bra and panty set.

Ellen had never been so mortified in her life.

She walked into the bar—shoulders back, coy smile, head up; think confident, be confident—and Will didn't even look at her. Yet he was standing right there.

"Will?"

He smiled. "Would you like a table?"

"No. I mean, I don't know. Are you off work yet?"

He looked confused and disconcerted. "Do I know . . . oh, we met at Cindy's party two weeks ago, right?"

"Yes. And we spoke on the phone? We were supposed to meet tonight after you'd finished work?"

His handsome face fell. "Ellen?"

"Yes."

"Oh, no. There's been a mistake." Holding her elbow, Will led Ellen to an empty table and gestured for her to sit. "I thought you were someone else. I thought you were blond."

It hit her like a toaster flung off a building. He thought Ellen was Helen—leggy, tall, tits on toast. She had also been at the party. Ellen remembered Will hanging by her side.

So. Has Ellen grown as a result of this encounter? No. She hasn't. It was a day not worth living.

*

DEAR SUE,

What is it about my ass?

I'm hiding in bed (I don't want to face my roommate just yet; there's honey all over the kitchen floor) surrounded by the detritus of last night. Twisted bra, dirty wineglasses, and one telling item—the DJ's watch.

Remember that guy I wrote you about last month?

The DJ? He's so cute, exactly my type. Shaggy hair, jeans that hug all the right places, tall, heroin thin, and obviously into music. I gave him my number. He didn't call. Finally, I just had to do it. I called him.

We went out last night.

I wasn't sure I'd recognize him, given my ragingly drunk status at the club that first night. So before hooking up at the restaurant, I drew on my old standby—liquid courage—and then met up with him. (I did recognize him, by the way. So don't start getting all interventiony. Yet.)

It was perfect: sitting with our legs entwined, talking about our shared hatred of Phish, faces moving closer and closer, staring into each other's eyes for eons. You know when your heart is pounding so hard you're sure he can see it through your shirt? And then he does that thing, that wonderful caveman thing—he grabs me by the back of the head and yanks me in for a kiss.

Boom! We're in a cab going back to my place, kissing like crazy. We were frantic and it was fantastic. (And no, I wasn't going to sleep with him. It was a first date. Give me some credit.)

Anyway, we're lying on my bed and he starts kissing my stomach. He moves lower. Nice. He takes my pants off and kisses my inner thighs. I'm enjoying this. Then, suddenly, he flips me over (for a skinny dude, this DJ's got pipes). So, he's kissing my ass—different, cool—and then I feel him part my cheeks. He's parting my *cheeks*! I guess he felt me stiffen or something, because he asks (a little late, in my opinion), "Do you mind if I lick your ass?"

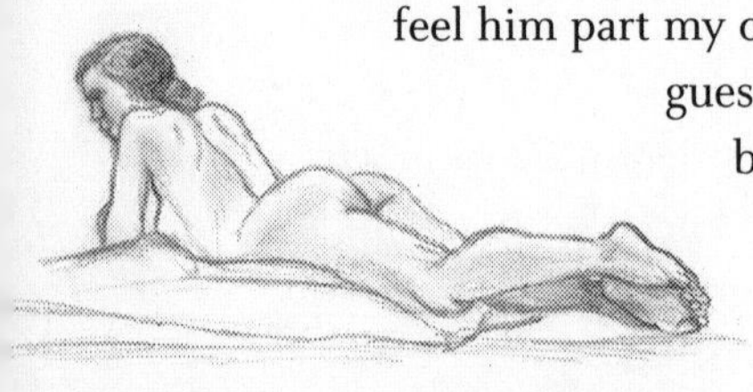

Do I mind? Um, yes. I scissored my legs shut and

said, "I don't think that's first-date material." He got huffy, implied that I was "anal" and left.

There was such promise, Sue. And then he had to go and focus on my bum. This is the third time a guy has headed buttward on a first date. And so I implore you to tell me: What is it about my ass?

Miss you,

Fanny

p.s. How are you?

❋

A MOVIE THEATRE, 1966.

Onscreen, the wife of a Kenyan game warden raises an orphaned lion cub named Elsa. In the back row of the theatre are Nancy and Charlie. It's a first date—he's a friend of a friend. Things are going well. They had a delicious dinner and are getting along well. Charlie suggested the movie, and Nancy was inclined to sit in the dark with him for a while.

She's not all that interested in the movie. Sure, it's based on a best-selling book and it's a true story, but an hour and thirty-five minutes is a long time to watch a lion.

As the woman raises the lioness to maturity, Charlie snuggles Nancy. She reaches for his hand. He holds it tightly. She shifts closer to him. He puts his head on her shoulder. Strange. She should be doing that to him. Nancy's never had a guy assume a feminine role before. Well, she's a modern woman. She can handle it and, really, it's quite nice. As long as he isn't too docile. She needs him to be a lion to her lioness. Nancy giggles.

Onscreen, the woman prepares Elsa for her return to the wild. Charlie says something, but it's muffled. Nancy turns to ask him to repeat it. She's shocked into silence. The man she thought was snuggling at her side for the entire movie is, in fact, weeping. "This is so sad," he cries.

That year, *Born Free* wins two Oscars for original music. The film also wins the media-based Laurel Award for Sleeper of the Year.

Nancy never sees Charlie again.

*

AFTER A CHORUS OF enthusiastic encouragement from her girlfriends, Joy caved. She e-mailed CLDBEYRS. She'd rejected a number of men on the online dating service: STALLION69 because of the posters of half-nude women on the walls behind him, and HORSECOOK because Joy suspected that was a deliberate typo.

"You can't base your opinion on his photo," sighed her best friend, Andrea. "You've got to actually chat with him. Besides, it's been a while. You can't afford to be picky."

CLDBEYRS looked cute in the photo, though it was fuzzy. And she wasn't sure about his moniker—did it mean "Could Be Yours" or "Could Be Years"? Maybe it's "Cold Beers"? Regardless, she e-mailed him and he e-mailed back and this continued for two weeks until she finally agreed to meet with him.

He seemed to have a sense of humour. He seemed to be kind. He seemed to be cute. She didn't know why she had agreed to meet him at his place—not the safest plan, but it was too late to back out. Besides, she didn't want him to know where her apartment was *and* Andrea's number was preprogrammed into her cellphone, just in case.

When CLDBEYRS opened the door to his high-rise apartment, Joy felt equal amounts of surprise and relief. He was taller than he'd said—six-one—and his picture didn't do him justice. Ushering her into his grubby apartment, Joy began taking stock but caught herself. She'd promised Andrea she'd give this guy a chance. She resolved to ignore the stale smell and his off-putting, long-jawed profile.

CLDBEYRS offered her a beer and then proposed a tour of the apartment. "I've been really looking forward to meeting you," he said. "And you're way sexier in person."

"Uh, thanks. Nice poster," Joy gestured to the gigantic *Tomb Raider* poster featuring Angelina Jolie in skin-tight shorts.

"Yeah. That's my favourite game," he said. "This is the bathroom." Joy saw wet towels on the floor and a gooey bar of soap with curly hair stuck all over it.

"God, you're beautiful," CLDBEYRS murmured.

Joy moved down the hall.

"This," said her date with a flourish, "is my bedroom."

It was the only clean room in the apartment. A pile of papers was stacked on the dresser, but other than that it was as close to spotless as CLDBEYRS seemed to get.

"Oh no," he said, putting his drink down on the bedside table. "I'm not feeling well at all. Whoa. Head rush."

Alarmed, Joy put her drink down and moved to help him sit on the bed. As she brushed past him, he fainted, grabbing her as he fell. The two collapsed on the bed.

CPR, she thought.

Struggling to get out of his iron grasp, Joy was startled when CLDBEYRS opened his eyes and smiled. "Hey, gorgeous," he said, pulling her so close she could smell his beery breath. "You know what would make me feel better? A kiss."

Using a well-positioned knee, Joy shoved him off of her and announced, "You're a pig," before gathering her things from the living room.

As she dialed Andrea's number from the elevator, she muttered to her reflection, "CLDBEYRS before I ever date again."

*

GRACE'S BOSS IS A RATHER GREASY SORT. His hair is perfectly trimmed at two inches and gelled to within an inch of its life. He wears suits that fit everywhere but his crotch. His considerable package, which Grace believes is enhanced with a pair of balled-up socks, pulls the fabric from the seat of his pants, causing a disconcerting ass outline. "You do know that you're not supposed to feel fabric *between* your cheeks," Grace came close to saying after he made a nasty comment about her sheer blouse.

He's also greasy in personality. Loving the fact that a hot, single, twenty-six-year-old is working for him, he makes sure to introduce her to every new client. "Grace will be working on your file. Very closely," he says with a leer.

When he slides into her office and compliments Grace on her hair, she knows it's bad news. She's right. He's decided to play matchmaker for Grace and a business client. "Tony is a valuable client," he says, fingering Grace's half-eaten sandwich. "I don't need to tell you that he's very important. And that means, very, very rich."

Grace, about to suggest that he shove his matchmaking where the sun don't shine, catches herself at "very rich." She's twenty-six. She likes baubles as much as the next girl. Who hasn't dreamed of her very own sugar daddy? Hell, why not?

Promptly at noon on Wednesday, Grace is waiting in front of the office for Tony to pick her up. She's picked out a beautiful dove-grey power suit, complete with a short, tight, tailored skirt that's currently the fashion. A light pink shirt and some pearl earrings and Grace is as ready as she'll ever be.

Surveying her reflection in the shop windows, Grace finds that, deep down, she's excited about the lunch. Tony, her boss said, is exactly her type, only a little older. That's fine. Grace has been known to daydream about a fit, trim forty-year-old man with a mysterious past. Her mind starts to drift.

That's when she hears the engine.

Pulling up to the curb is a cherry-red Ferrari with tinted windows. It jerks to a stop right beside her and the engine is cut. The door opens and out steps a man who weighs at least three hundred pounds and is not a day less than seventy-five.

❋

THIRTY-EIGHT MONTHS. Claire's been single for thirty-eight long, dry, unhappy months. In a rare display of grrrl power, Claire signs up with two online dating services. She screens potential dates until the men meet, at the very least, her top five criteria: income ($70,000+), age (forty-six to fifty-four), status (single), sexual orientation (straight), and criminal record (none). For four months, she plans three dates every other weekend in the fervent hope that she'll find a match.

After yet another disappointing date, Claire's friend Emma sets her up. Ethan has a similar education and is in Claire's financial bracket. After a quick conversation on the phone, they meet at a local bar, shoehorning each other in between work and dinner.

"So, Emma tells me that you love sex," says Ethan, after ordering drinks. "My place isn't too far from here. I can easily cancel my dinner."

"Wow. That's direct," she hedges, noting that Emma must be killed. "I'm pretty choosy about who I sleep with these days. I'd like to get to know you a bit better, if that's okay."

"Yeah, sure. No problem. My ex-wife was like that, too. Wouldn't give it up for three months at first. I think maybe she's frigid, because she stopped wanting it after we got married."

Over the next ten minutes, Claire tries not to gulp her dry white wine as Ethan talks about his rotten ex-wife. He turns to his "amazing" and "fulfilling" volunteer work (walking dogs for the SPCA) and the joys of golf.

"I'll teach you to play," he says to Claire. "You'll love it. Great! That's settled."

"Thanks," says Claire, "but I know how to play and I'm actually not all that keen on it."

"No, no. You like golf," insists Ethan. "And I'll teach you how to play properly. Not many people really know how to play the game the way it's supposed to be played. You sure you don't want to have sex?"

"Yes."

"Right. Well, golfing—"

"I'm sorry, I have to go," says Claire, putting on her jacket and grabbing her purse. "Really nice to meet you. Great. Fun."

"You'll love golf," says Ethan. "And maybe next time we can have sex."

❊

A LIST OF MISTAKES

1. When an old acquaintance from high school (whom I haven't spoken to in years) calls out of the blue to ask if I would go out with a friend of hers called Bob, I say, "Sure."
2. When, a few days later, Bob calls, I agree to go out on a Saturday night despite my best instincts.
3. I've never met this man, but I agree to have dinner with him even though it means at least three hours spent in his company.
4. I agree to eat at a "family restaurant."
5. I actually show up.
6. I stay, even when I finally meet Bob, who is five-three and wearing black shiny pants, referee shoes, and a grey corduroy blazer with elbow patches like those of a university prof from the 1960s.

7. I continue to stay put even after I order wine, only to hear Bob tell the waitress he never drinks and can't understand why other people do.
8. I ask him about what sort of television he watches. "Well," says Bob, "on Mondays, at seven, I tape ya-da-ya-da and, at eight, I tape so-and-so. On Tuesdays, I tape ya-da-ya-da, this-and-that, and blah-blah-blah. On Wednesdays, I tape. . . ."

    I got the whole week's lineup. "That's a lot of television," I say. "When do you watch them?"

    "On the weekends," he says.
9. Having made Mistake No. 8, I ask Bob about his favourite kind of films. "I like really realistic films," he says. Is there a glimmer of some artistic depth here?

    "Like what?"

    "Oh, I can't really say."

    "Come on, you must have one or two favourites."

    "Well," Bob pauses for a moment. "I really like *The Sound of Music*."
10. Not leaving when the bill arrives and Bob gets into a heated debate with the waitress because she won't accept an out-dated coupon he has for the restaurant. (After a discussion with the manager, Bob is permitted to use his coupon.)
11. Not escaping when Bob disappears into the washroom for twenty minutes.
12. Not throttling Bob when he goes over the bill again and starts to add up the numbers, moving his lips and looking at the ceiling. He calls the waitress back and asks her if the "math" is correct.

A LIST OF ACCOMPLISHMENTS

1. After Bob finally pays the bill, he asks me if I want to get a drink (reminding me that he'll just have coffee) and I say I have an early meeting. I'm home at 9:50 p.m.

2. When, a few days later, I get home from work and there's the following message on my machine: "Hi, it's Bob. Remember me? I had such a wonderful time; I'd love to get together again. Call me," I don't.
3. When, the very next day, I get home from work and there's the following message: "Hi, it's Bob. I haven't heard from you. I really had a wonderful time and I'd love to get together to play tennis or go biking or go rollerblading or hiking or play badminton or go bowling or play baseball or volleyball or really anything! Call me," I don't.
4. When, a week later, I get home from work and there's the following message on my machine from the "friend" who set us up: "I just spoke to Bob. He raved about your date. He really wants to go out with you again. You should," I don't call her back either.

❋

ONCE UPON A TIME, Abigail adored a boy. At sixteen, she'd dated a few guys, but Mike was the eighteen-year-old brother of a friend and *totally* mature. One day, while hanging out in the kitchen at her friend's house, Abigail was surprised to see Mike heading straight for her. Straightening her shoulders, she gave him a bright smile. "Wanna go out on Friday?" he asked.

"Sure," she replied.

He nodded and then went to the shed to tinker with his car.

By Friday afternoon, Abigail hadn't heard another peep from Mike and was sick with worry. What if he doesn't ever call? What if he forgot? What if he decided he doesn't like me after all? And then she thought of something even more worrying: What if he actually shows up?

At eight, a car honked outside her home. It was Mike. Abigail grabbed her coat and purse and yelled goodbye to her parents.

"When will you be back?" they asked.

"Later," she answered.

Abigail hopped into the car and Mike suggested that they go to Bogden Point. During the week, the cliff offered a gorgeous view of the ocean. On weekends, the dense forest and lack of lighting appealed to a younger generation. Abigail agreed, and off they went.

Mike found a spot to park. There was an awkward silence. "What do you wanna do?" asked Abigail.

"Make out," replied Mike.

And make out they did.

About the time that the car windows steamed up, Abigail reached for Mike's zipper. He groaned. Slowly, she pulled it down. He kissed her harder. Abigail—being of the mind that any girl who wanted to keep her reputation and still be asked out was no stranger to the art of a hand job—reached inside Mike's pants. He shifted. She touched. He sighed. She fumbled. He stiffened.

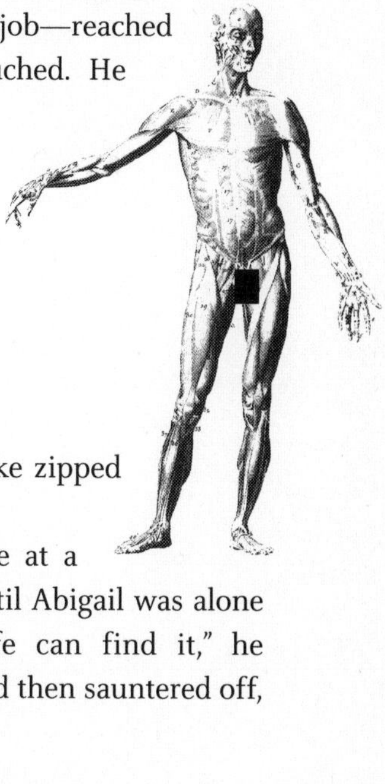

"Um, where is it?" she asked.

"What?"

"Your thing. I can't find it."

"You've got it. Right now."

"Really?"

"Yes."

"Oh."

Abigail slowly withdrew her hand. Mike zipped up his pants.

Years later, Abigail bumped into Mike at a party. There with his wife, Mike waited until Abigail was alone and then marched up to her. "My wife can find it," he announced. Mike looked at her carefully and then sauntered off, leaving Abigail choking on crudités.

She had dressed with more than usual care, and prepared in the highest spirits for the conquest of all that remained unsubdued of his heart, trusting that it was not more than might be won in the course of the evening.

JANE AUSTEN, *Pride and Prejudice*, 1813

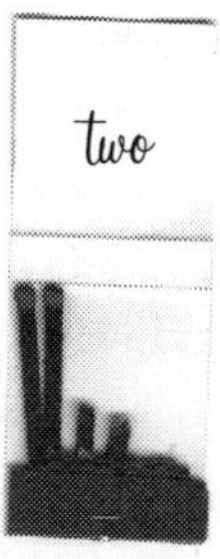

Isn't This Special?

THE BRIDAL BOUQUET is coming straight at me.

I'm at a wedding on Prince Edward Island. The church is gorgeous. Swags of ivy and ribbon decorate the wooden pews. The service is a nail-biter because the minister, old and dotty, forgets the bride's name. The groom is my boyfriend's best friend. This event is a big deal for my boyfriend. Not only is he the master of ceremonies but he's excited about his friends all finally meeting his girlfriend. Me.

I, on the other hand, have been worried about this wedding—will his friends like me? Will I have to spend most of it alone as he does his MC thing? Will I meet a bitchy ex-girlfriend? Will people ask when we're going to get married?

I needn't have worried. His friends are wonderful, embracing me as one of their own. The food is delicious. No bitchy ex-girlfriends in attendance. The reception is lovely—held in an old barn on the property of a gorgeous resort. But here we are. My least favourite moment of any wedding. The bouquet toss.

"C'mon, single ladies," urged my boyfriend just moments ago. "Get out on the dance floor with your catcher's mitts." Jostling each other in their hurry to find the right position are women as old as forty and as young as eleven. I'm hiding behind one of the posts decorated in hearts and garlands.

"Amy? Where are you? Get out here," boomed my boyfriend into the mic. "Okay, folks, my girlfriend seems to be a bit shy. Tall, curly blond hair. Probably blushing. Anyone know where she is? Amy?"

Someone's nasty old uncle, cake crumbs flecking his chin, shoves me onto the dance floor, which is how I now find myself the target of the bridal bouquet.

I see the crowd of women in front of me, turning to stare at who will catch the bouquet. Lips tight with disappointment, cheeks pink with embarrassment, eyes gleaming with amusement. The delicate pink roses, the baby's breath, and the trails of ivy make a beautiful, high arc across the room. Women are straining for it, snapping their fingers at ribbons just beyond their grasp. My boyfriend—still holding the microphone—watches the floral trajectory. There's hope on his face.

I hear him call my name in encouragement. I look at the bouquet. A heavy-set divorcee falls to the ground, slipping on the polished floor. A finger brushes the stems, twisting the bouquet just enough so that it veers directly toward my chest. It's like a freakin' homing pigeon. Everything moves in slow motion. I won't have to stretch to grab it. I can smell the roses. It's right in front of my face. It's falling into my hands, only my hands aren't there. Where are my hands? By my side? What are they doing there? Lift them. Catch this bloody thing. That's the right thing to do. That's the *only* thing to do.

The bouquet crashes to my feet. I stare at it. The room is hushed. Nothing happens. Mouths gape. I'm frozen. A young woman in a canary-yellow dress that's a size too big asks me if I'm going to pick it up. I look at her in terror.

"Why don't I just take it, then?" she says. Bending down, she plucks the flowers from my toes.

"I guess that answers my question," my boyfriend says as the music starts up.

❋

WAKE. EAT. SHOWER. PEE. Commute. Work. Coffee. Eat. Commute. Eat. Shit. Sleep. Repeat ad nauseam. Most days, we do this by rote. Not to make us sound like automatons. We like our routines. However, a special occasion is, by definition, a day that's out of the ordinary. Forget your long and lean jeans and flip-flops; this is a Miu Miu knock-off, spray-on tan, get-your-hair-done day. Everything is heightened—secrecy, emotions, and expectations. You plan big. Dream big.

On a special occasion, you're given leave to go wild. Wear that gorgeous black sequined dress you bought on a whim. The neckline might be dangerous but, dammit, you look like a firecracker. While you're at it, toss on Grandma's diamond studs. Book a reservation at the most frou-frou joint in town. Withdraw lots of money from your savings account. Hell, go into overdraft if you like. You only live once.

This is the time we plan extravagant declarations of love and destiny. The time for big gestures. In high school, that meant personalized T-shirts and heart-shaped pizzas on Valentine's Day with a card that reads "When the moon hits your eye like a big pizza pie, that's *amore*." Now that we're older, gestures more often take the form of iPods and tickets to *Mamma Mia*.

By far, the best part of a special occasion is that tiny, perfect, fragile bubble of hope. The moment when you think, *Something perfect might happen today.* To date, perchance to dream. Alas. . . .

❄

FEBRUARY 15, 2001, 1:33 A.M.

Okay. I thought a first date scheduled for Valentine's Day was pretty intense. But I was, I must admit, swayed by George's German accent. I love accents (German's not my top pick but, really, any accent will do). Anyway, he sounded nice and had the restaurant all picked out. Why not, right? So, I meet him at this cool Chinese–French fusion place. Great food, great ambience. And George, being German, is tall, blond, and handsome. I'm digging this date.

We start off with small talk. We're laughing, even flirting a little, but an hour into the date he starts to pepper me with questions. Not just any questions. Weird questions. "How do you feel about zee public tranzportashun?" Uh, good. "Do you like paintings in vatercolours or oils?" Oils are nice.

Mr. Twenty Questions isn't taken with my answers because just after our soba noodles with stir-fried pineapple and rare hoisin duck breast arrives, he puts down his chopsticks. "I am sorry, but vee are not getting along." I sit there, dumb. Then he folds his napkin and announces, "Zee date is over." People are staring. That's all he says. That's it. He gets up, grabs his coat, offers me a short bow good night—a *bow*—and leaves.

Never forget a friend,
especially if he owes you.
Lucky Numbers 4, 5, 9, 15, 28, 29

Part of me actually finds this funny. I mean, vone must admire a man who is *zat* direct. I cannot, however, forgive him for leaving me to pick up the tab.

Thank God for Jen and Kath. They call my cellphone as I'm doggy bagging the meal and drag me off to Souz Dal for martinis. Jen has just escaped a date with a manic nail-biter who hates his mother. So we eat hoisin duck from a bag under the table, laughing and drinking our dates away.

A quiet evening with friends is the best tonic for a long day.
Lucky Numbers 6, 11, 14, 22, 24, 35

Now I'm lying in bed with the Souz Dal bartender. *Plus ça change. . . .*

❋

"MADDY! HOW DID THE BIG DATE GO?"

"Oh, Jen, it was awful."

"Why? What happened?"

"Okay. I plan this gorgeous dinner, right? For our one-month anniversary. And I know that's cheesy, so please don't get all over me about it again. It was special. Supposed to be special—Josh has never been to my place before and so it was—"

"Your chance to show off how great a cook, housekeeper, and lover you could be?"

"Yes."

"Go on."

"So, he arrives. And he's brought me a bunch of beautiful flowers. Daisies. I take his coat and go into the kitchen to get him a glass of wine. I'm pouring the wine when I hear him yell, 'Shit!' from the living room. Jen—Gus bit him."

"No. Seriously?"

"Yeah, my stupid, stupid dog. . . ."

"Whose good manners were supposed to be a reflection of the kind of mother you'll make."

"Exactly. That mutt just chomped Josh's hand."

"Blood?"

"No. Thank God."

"What did you do?"

"I smacked his bum."

"Isn't that a bit forward for a one-month anniversary?"

"Ha ha. So, we have dinner. Everything's fine."

"There's more?"

"Yes. It gets worse. I didn't burn anything and Gus seems to be accepting Josh, sniffing his pants and lying at his feet. And by then he'd stopped growling whenever Josh moved."

"Why didn't you put Gus in the bedroom or something?"

"Jen, my dog has to get along with my boyfriend. I can't always lock Gus up whenever Josh comes over. Anyway, we're cuddling on the couch after dinner. Josh is stroking my leg and I'm resting my head on his shoulder. It's lovely. Just like I imagined. Then Gus jumps up and settles on Josh's lap. It's perfect."

"Oh, good. So they got along eventually."

"No. After a couple of minutes, Gus jumps down, runs off, and Josh says, 'Your dog just shat on my lap.'"

"No! Maddy."

"Yeah. So we're over. One month. Done."

"What? Why? I'm sure it wasn't that big of a deal for Josh."

"You don't understand. I can't date Josh any more. It's over. My dog doesn't like him. That's it."

"I think what Gus was trying to tell you is not to celebrate a one-month anniversary."

"I hate you."

*

IT'S SUZETTE'S TWENTY-FIRST BIRTHDAY.

Two weeks ago, lovely Les asked her out. A big, burly guy with crinkles around his eyes, Les is a friend of one of Suzette's co-workers. Recently, she'd gotten to know him better. He lives in her area and she's bumped into him twice. He was walking his dog, Lady, and she liked the way he said hello to the other dog walkers. A nod and a smile. When she saw him in a T-shirt for the first time two weeks ago, Suzette had goosebumps. Not only are his arms stacked but on his right bicep is a tattoo of what she learned is an Indian symbol for joy.

When Les asked her out, Suzette told him that the day he'd picked was her birthday. "Excellent," he said. "I'll make it even more special."

Yes, please, thinks Suzette.

On the day of her birthday, Suzette gets up early for a manicure appointment. While at the spa, she also waxes her bikini line and splurges on a pedicure. *What the hell,* she thinks, and tints her eyelashes. After treating herself to a nice lunch, she goes home to dress for her date with Les.

Pink linen sundress. New white cardigan. Pale yellow and pink purse with lipstick, money, keys, and cellphone. Outrageously expensive strappy pink sandals that she bought a few days earlier. While spritzing perfume in her cleavage, the doorbell rings.

"Happy birthday, Suze." Les kisses her cheek. She's never liked *Suze*, but coming from his plump, kissable lips, Suzette's inclined to reconsider. "You look fabulous," he tells her. "Ready to go? I've got everything planned."

Les opens the door of his Firebird muscle car. Suzette tries not to notice the baby-blue garter hanging from the rear-view mirror. Les slides behind the wheel. "First stop," he says, beaming, "monster truck show."

Suzette giggles until Les looks at her, puzzled.

"Are you serious?" she asks.

"Yeah."

"Oh. Sounds great."

Twenty minutes later, Suzette picks her way across wooden boards that serve as flooring in the arena. She's assaulted by the smell of car oil, the sound of engines roaring to life, and the crush of bodies. Les buys her a hot dog and a beer and then finds them seats in the stands.

Surely this is just to throw me off, thinks Suzette. *Dinner and movie. That's all I wanted.*

After two hours of spectacular crashes, Suzette turns to Les. "I'm losing my hearing," she says. "Can we go?"

"Sure, babe," says Les. "I didn't realize you weren't having fun."

Before going to the car, Suzette ducks into the ladies' room to check her makeup and adjust her dress. She doesn't want to frighten the maître d' at whatever restaurant they're going to.

"Next stop," says Les, starting the car, "is a surprise."

When he drives past the city limits, Suzette is alarmed. "Where are we going?" she asks.

"It's a surprise," say Les. "Don't worry. You'll love it."

After forty-five minutes on the road, Suzette is annoyed. "Where are we going, Les? I mean it. Where?"

"Funny you should ask," he answers. "We're here."

Suzette looks out the window. Les pulls into a farmer's field, past a handmade sign advertising *Drag Race Parking.*

"We're going drag racing?" Suzette screeches. "You're taking me drag racing?"

"No, no, no," he assures her. "We're not going to drag race. We're going to *watch* the races."

Suzette is home at midnight. Her linen dress is splattered with mud and the heel on one shoe has snapped. Her white cardigan is ruined. She lost her purse. Her face is streaked with tears.

"Can I come in?" asks Les at her door.

"I have a little surprise for you," says Suzette, as she slams the door behind her.

❄

WHAT'S HIS NAME? *Brian? Brent? I think it starts with a* B *but maybe a* D. *What's his goddamn name?*

Dierdre is late. Half-jogging down the sidewalk in high heels and a suit, she's also in a full panic. First, she'd almost forgotten that her friend arranged this blind date and, second, she can't remember her date's name.

Fumbling in her purse for her cellphone, Dierdre calls her friend. "Hi, you've reached Tanya's cell," the recording kicks in. "Leave a message after the. . . ." *Beep.*

"Hey T, it's me. I'm on my way to meet your Ultimate friend but I've totally blanked on his name. Can you call me back as soon as you get this and, if I'm already there, just say his name and then hang up, 'kay?"

David? Darren? Damian?

Wheeling into the pub, Dierdre spots her date right away. He's a redhead and there's no mistaking him in the bar filled with blonds and brunettes.

"Hi," she thrusts her hand out. "I'm Dierdre."

"It's great to meet you," he says. "You okay? You look like you were running."

"Oh, no, no. Just didn't want to be too late."

Shit. He didn't say his name. Maybe I could just ask him. That's okay, isn't it? All right, I'm going to ask him. Dierdre opens her mouth.

"So, Dierdre," begins her date. "I've been looking forward to this. Tanya's told me a lot about you."

He got my name right. That never happens. People always pronounce it "deerdree" instead of "deerdra." Crap. Can I still ask? Why isn't Tanya calling?

"Tell me about the music business," her date prompts.

As Dierdre talks about her work at a record company, she

scrambles to think of a way to get him to say his name.

"And so, I can just pitch the lyrics or the whole package," she blathers. "Now, tell me about you. Did you have a nickname growing up?"

He shoots her a strange look and then answers, "No. Did you?"

"Uh, no. What about clients? As an accountant, do you let them call you by your first name?"

"Depends. If they want to, sure. I don't have any problem with that."

"Oh."

For the next hour, Dierdre keeps trying to bring up subjects that require him to use his name. Finally, he excuses himself to go to the washroom.

The second he turns the corner, Dierdre pounces on his briefcase. *Dammit. Locked. Wait, his wallet is in the jacket hanging on the back of the chair.*

Reaching across the table, Dierdre fishes in the inner pocket and grabs his wallet. She's pulling out his driver's licence when she hears, "What are you doing with my wallet?"

Dierdre wants to die. What is she going to tell him? Not the truth. They've been talking for over an hour now. It's too late to ask him his effing name.

"Um, I couldn't believe that you're only thirty-three. I mean, you look so much younger and I just wanted to, you know, check. Besides, I wanted to find out what your sign is."

"Taurus. But you could've asked," he says, grabbing the wallet out of her sweaty grasp.

"Then we're compatible." Having never read a horoscope in her life, Dierdre forces a smile.

"Can I see the licence again?" she asks, desperate. "I want to see your picture."

Her date stares at her and hands over his licence.

Steve. His name is Steve. A wave of relief washes over her. Now she can enjoy his company instead of acting like a maniac.

"Dierdre," he says. Steve keeps pronouncing her name correctly. Maybe it's a sign. Maybe it's fate. Maybe this is a funny story she can tell their grandkids.

Maybe not.

Steve tucks the licence back into his wallet and leaves, informing Dierdre that he's looking for someone a little more relaxed.

It takes more than good memory
to have good memories.
Lucky Numbers 4, 18, 26, 28, 34, 43

❋

MAY 1984.

Prom night, minus 120 hours.

Still no date for the prom. Dad keeps offering. Thinks it's funny. Maybe contract chicken pox?

* * *

Prom night, minus seventy-one hours.

Have bit bullet and told Lara and Shaelyn am definitely not going to prom. No date. Can't face it stag even though Mom and Dad bought dream dress they can't afford. Aqua blue, satin, off the shoulder. A waste.

* * *

Prom night, minus forty-six hours.

Lara called. Knows someone who needs a date. Nice guy from another school. Has set it up already, so am going with guy named Trevor. *Trevor.* At least it's not Dad. Am looking pale. Maybe should tan tomorrow?

* * *

Prom night, minus twenty-two hours.

Am bright red. Have burned skin to crisp. Not only burned, but tan line is crooked! Most embarrassing moment: Mom patting aloe all over my *naked* body. Says it'll be fine for tomorrow night.

* * *

Prom night, minus twenty-one hours.

Good freaking God. Dress neckline is lower than bright-red burn line. Triangle of lily-white skin right above boobs. Heavier foundation?

* * *

Prom night, minus twelve hours.

Oh. My. God. Have six cold sores on lips. *Six!!!!* Am going to die. Forgot to put aloe on lips. Committing hara-kiri now. Goodbye world.

* * *

Prom night, minus eleven hours.

Forbidden to commit suicide by Lara. Trevor is ready and "totally psyched." Lara claims no one will notice sores. Has a trick to cover up acne and so will come over before prom to perform magic on lips and tan line.

* * *

Prom night, minus two minutes.

Dad home from work. Response to oozing, gross lips on daughter: "Jesus, Mary, and Joseph! What have you been eating? Dead squirrel?" This *after* Lara performed "magic." Mom nearly killed him. Can't go through with this. Lara says Trevor won't notice, but acting weird. Keeps disappearing to use phone in basement.

* * *

Prom night, minus ten minutes.

Might throw up. At least not genuine burn victim.

* * *

Prom night, plus six hours.

Am never speaking to Lara/Shaelyn again.

Lara was right. Trevor doesn't say anything about cold sores or burn. Get to dance. Everyone staring. "Quite the burn ya got there." "What's on yer lip?"

Trevor is nice. Dance and leave for beach party. Trevor goes in other car. Makes out with other girl in other car. Am with Lara. Get lost. Can't find party. Finally find party. Bitchface, a.k.a. Lucy, says, "So, had to buy a date, eh? You could've at least found someone a little older."

Find Trevor. Demand answers. He goes red. Tells me that he's *two years* younger!! Friend of Lara's brother. Was *paid* $30 by so-called friends to be my date.

Come home crying. Dad makes popcorn and sets up a movie. Tells me I am gorgeous, strong woman. Stupid, but makes me feel better.

To travel hopefully is a better thing than to arrive.

ROBERT LOUIS STEVENSON,
Virginibus Puerisque, "El Dorado," 1881

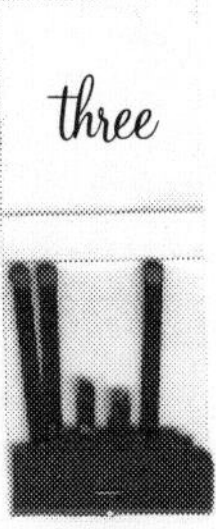

three

A Broad Abroad

I WAS EIGHTEEN YEARS OLD, attending my final year of high school in the south of France and living in my first home *sans* parents, which I shared with two other girls from the Lycée. Our tiny apartment (we were supposed to live with the hosting French families, but our Madame didn't want *les canadiennes débraillées* living in her beautiful sixteenth-century home, so they rented us a separate space) was right in the heart of Villefranche-sur-Mer, a thirteenth-century coastal fishing village just outside Nice. Off our kitchen was a small terrace that overlooked the sea and, from one corner of the garden, if I craned my neck while standing on the old stone wall, I could see the beach where I had learned to sunbathe nude. The beach where I had kissed Pete.

The Lycée was a Canadian high school—the teachers were Canadian and so were all sixty or so students. The cost was steep; most parents scratched together what they could to pay for this amazing experience during which their precious children would learn French. And we did learn some of the language. I'll never forget, for example, that *cornichons* is the word for gherkins, while *nichons* means nipples. I also now know better than to try to engage a French baker in a debate over why French bread is better than Canadian bread—*préservatif,* I found out, does not mean in French what it sounds like in English. (Until someone overheard our conversation and corrected me, I was apparently talking about Canadian bread containing too many condoms for it to be truly tasty. The baker was understandably appalled.)

So, we learned to order food, read train schedules to Monaco, and ask for directions to the casino. But, truth be told, we really learned about freedom.

For the first three months we were in France, the Lycée students tested new-found wings. We stayed out until dawn. We drank enormous bottles of cheap, red plonk that was called wine but tasted like rotten grapes mixed with rubbing alcohol. We took off our clothes and ran naked into the sea. We slept through morning classes. And we dated a different person, usually a classmate, every week.

From the first day, I'd had my eye on Peter. He was tall, slim, and had shaggy blond hair that fell into his eyes. Personable and funny, he'd charmed a number of girls in those first few weeks. So when I found myself walking along the beach with him one balmy October evening, I thought the world was my *huître.* Here I was in France! On a beach, drinking wine! With a delicious guy holding my hand! In that moment, I could feel my world expand.

The Kiss

We found a secluded spot on the beach and sat down. I'd never been much of a drinker but the wine, while not smooth, became easier to swallow with every swig from the brown paper bag. Pete and I chatted about nothing and everything. The moon was big and beautiful, its light casting us in a soft, silver glow. We leaned in, at exactly the same moment, and kissed. It was perfect. Life was perfect.

Our kiss ended. We smiled into each other's eyes. I turned away from his lips and threw up in his lap.

*

THE LURE OF TRAVELLING is in its weightlessness. Stepping on that plane or train, you leave behind jobs, family, mortgages, and friends. Life becomes lighter and, as a result, more fun to play or mould into whatever shape pleases you best. Stepping off the plane or train in a new city or country, you're surrounded by people who don't know you, and any lingering inhibitions are shed. A shy, awkward woman swings her hips and sings karaoke. An outgoing clown becomes a brooding artist. The Respectable Girl becomes the Shameless Hussy.

Anything is possible when travelling and, especially in romance, anything goes. At home, you describe your type as a single male, six-two or taller, two hundred pounds or less, with a disposable income, a sense of humour, a car, and preferably a Ph.D. Abroad, you can be honest and choose the hunky blonds with promising packages and ignore the fact that they confuse Iran with Iraq.

1000

[a promising package]

*

ON A COLD, DREARY AUTUMN DAY, midway through Lisa's university career, she makes a solemn vow. Surrounded by books, binders, paper, unpaid bills, and a chipped coffee cup filled with last night's brew, Lisa promises to graduate magna cum laude and treat herself to a summer of backpacking through Europe.

Already an excellent student, Lisa is pretty sure she can accomplish her goal.

Over the next two years, whenever Lisa is drowning in a sea of library books while studying for exams or pulling an all-nighter to finish an essay on Nietzsche, she thinks of Europe. "French men, Italian men, sun, salt water." This is her mantra.

She saves money and plans her itinerary. She studies. She works. She buys a high-end digital camera. She graduates—magna cum laude. Europe is calling.

Packing her knapsack with care (even should she buy a leather coat in Florence, it still won't weigh more than forty-five pounds), Lisa says goodbye to her parents and catches her flight to London. Over the next four weeks, she visits Paris, Cannes, Barcelona, Milan, and Florence. It's everything she'd dreamed of and she's giddy with happiness. She's also snap happy. So far, her favourite photos are of nude sunbathers picking each other's pimples, a perky museum guide smoking a joint on her break, and a child crying in front of Gaudí's Casa Batllò. She debates whether to go to Rome (think of the possibilities: tourists tumbling down the Spanish Steps, hot dog vendors at the Coliseum), but runs out of time.

On her way back to London, Lisa stops in Switzerland. The student hostel is located at the base of two mountains, with tiny, twee cottages housing the guests. Known for its hiking trails and spectacular view, this hostel is perfect for Lisa, who's grown tired of the big-city bustle.

In the crux of the mountains is a powerful waterfall. The view is like nothing she's ever seen before.

The evening after her arrival, Lisa heads to the bar in the main hostel. She shoots a couple of Red Bull and vodkas and strikes up a conversation with Jon, an Australian tour bus driver. He's young, cute, and very nice. He does this amazing trick with his tongue where he turns it into a clover shape. Plus, Lisa digs his accent.

A couple more vodka shooters later and they start dancing. They chicken dance. They samba. They disco. Lisa can't stop giggling. Puffing from a vigorous two-step, Jon suggests a moonlit stroll by the waterfall. The scene is idyllic: a full moon hanging above two dark mountains, its light sparkling on the water.

Jon leads Lisa back to his cottage. He pours her a Scotch and holds her gaze for a second longer than necessary. They kiss. Jon takes the glass from her hand and places it on the table. They touch. She's in a daze. Everything feels so good.

Around five in the morning, Lisa snuggles into Jon's side. He's fallen into a heavy sleep and she can't help thinking how romantic this evening's been—exactly like a drugstore romance novel, complete with heaving bosom, throbbing manhood, and pulses racing as they made love all over the tiny Swiss cottage. A full moon blessing the unlikely union of a dashing Australian and a bookish Canadian. The wild yet calming rush of a waterfall.

Wait. The sound of running water is much louder than it was before. Lisa sits up and peers toward the window. Then, looking down at the mattress, she confirms her suspicions. "You're peeing." She smacks Jon on the hip. "You are peeing. In bed."

Jon, half asleep, turns his head toward her and purrs, "Baby, that ain't pee." Lisa is no longer tipsy enough to find this amusing, especially as her leg is soaked in urine and starting to itch. She smacks him again and Jon wakes up. He takes a deep breath, glances at his now deflated manhood, and agrees: "Yeah, I'm peeing."

Lisa stumbles back to her cabin. "No one ever has to know about this," she mutters. "I'm in a different country. It's okay. As far as I'm concerned, I've never had a golden shower."

In her Europe photo album, there's only one shot from Switzerland: the tail end of a tour bus driving down the mountain.

*

FROM: Sara
DATE: Monday, April 19, 2004 4:19PM
TO: Amy
RE: Humiliation

Prague, 1973.

I'm twenty-one and travelling on my own.

I can't find a room in this city and I keep running into this very cute black-market money-changer. "I give you best rate for dollar," he says, smiling at me. He's wearing blue jean coveralls—the height of fashion back then—and clogs. Everyone else in Prague is wearing dreary polyester pants and plastic shoes.

At around 8 p.m., I run into him for the third time that day. I'm desperate to find a room, but he tells me, "Don't worry, we'll go to bar and see if my friend can help."

We go to quite a few bars. No friend in sight.

I'm getting rather merry, as is he. At some point, we start necking. I'm thinking, "At last, I can be promiscuous." (I'd been with just one guy since I was nineteen and felt I was missing out on all the zipless fucks out there.)

Finally, it's getting really late and my money-changer says, "I know where we can go."

He leads me through the streets and then through a dark doorway. We stumble upstairs to a small apartment. We don't turn on any lights, we just fumble toward the bed, which is sitting in what looks like the living room. I can't see anything, really. There are vague shapes—a chair, a bookshelf, and a mound of clothes or pillows on the other side of the room.

The combination of booze and lust is powerful and we have a wild and noisy time. Though I've never been a screamer, I decide to try it out that night. "Yeah, baby. That's it. More. Yeah. Oh, oh, oh. OHHHHHHH!!!!" Then we sleep.

In the woozy morning, I open my eyes and look around the room. We *are* in the living room. I can now clearly see the chair and bookshelf I noticed last night. I look at the mound. The mound is moving.

I'm thinking that it's an enormous rat and am about to scream bloody murder when I realize that the mound is a middle-aged woman waking up. The mound is his mother. I kid you not.

She was sweet and made breakfast for us, though all I could do was hope to God that she was a very heavy sleeper.

✻

HANDS HIDING HER NAKED BREASTS, Abigail bursts into the room of her hostel. Red-faced and out of breath, she slams the door behind her and collapses on the bed in a cloud of dust.

Her hair is a wild nest, filled with bits of dry leaves and small branches. Her jean shorts are brown with dust and dirt. Thin red scratches cover her arms, back, and chest.

What a night.

Rolling over on the bed, Abigail reaches for a shirt from her backpack.

It is only then—one hand in her backpack, her heart calming, her breath returning to normal—that Abigail starts to giggle.

How did I end up here?

For the last month, Abigail backpacked her way through France and Italy, exploring the history of cities during the day and the mysteries of men at night. She is currently checking out Greece.

The same afternoon that she arrived in Athens, Abby met a Dutch boy named Dirk who is also on a summer trip. You know that old saying "hot as Dutch love"? It's true. Dirk is so yummy, in fact, that she postpones her departure by four days. They dirty dance at a cheesy club, buy each other leather thongs to tie back their long hair, and ramble through local meat markets, taking photographs of the butchered pigs hanging from rusty meathooks.

On their final night together, Dirk wants to surprise Abigail with a "special date." He picks her up at eight and takes her for dinner at a local restaurant they discovered together earlier in the week. Then Dirk leads Abby through the dark and empty leather market and up the hill to the Acropolis.

"Isn't it closed?" she whispers, as they approach the ticket booth.

"A love as powerful as ours can break any lock." He kisses her. "I want to make love to you on the Parthenon. I want to see your body bathed in the lights of history."

Dirk fancies himself a poet.

Access to the ancient site ended more than two hours before. They jiggle the gates, contemplate climbing them, and then Dirk pulls her into the brush beside the ticket booth.

"We'll find another spot. We'll rely on the gods to lead us to Nature's bed."

Lust goggles prevent Abby from snorting.

Stumbling along the hill, the lovers find a spot overlooking the Theatre of Dionysus. *How cool is that?* Abby thinks. *Screwing a sex god while the god of sex watches? Okay, the god of wine . . . but wine always leads to sex.*

Dirk drags her to the ground, grinding his hips into hers. They fumble with shirts, tearing them from sweaty skin.

"I wanna do you. Now," moans Dirk, scrambling to pull off his pants. The best part about making out with Dirk, Abby has discovered, is that he drops the poet act.

Dirk reaches for Abby's zipper when a sound stops them. Dogs. Big dogs barking.

Peering over Dirk's shoulder, Abigail sees flashlights bobbing in the night and the silhouettes of two large dogs racing toward them.

"Shit. Guards," she hisses. "Get off."

Bounding to her feet, Abby wastes no time sliding down the hill. She hears yelling, but doesn't stop. No passport, no Greek, and a ticket booked for tomorrow morning's ferry—no *way* is she spending her last night in jail.

As Abigail passes under the first street lamp at the bottom of the hill, she realizes she's forgotten to grab her shirt. *Maybe Dirk has it.*

Moving into the shadows, Abby waits for Dirk to catch up. When he doesn't show up, she gets nervous and decides to return to the hostel. Hands holding her breasts (for support and modesty's sake), Abigail runs through the streets of Athens, ducking into shadows or shrubs at any sign of life. As she ducks and bobs and scampers, Abigail is consumed with one thought.

Where is Dirk?

Dirk, as it turns out, is caught with his pants down.

Half an hour after Abigail finally yanks a T-shirt over her head, Dirk shuffles into the hostel room. "I've never known such fear," he says. "My pants were twisted around my ankles. I couldn't get away. The guards found me. It was torture. Awful."

Had he just been caught pissing, Dirk explains, there wouldn't have been any trouble. Among men, that sort of thing is understood. Unfortunately, the sound of Abby crashing down the hill alerted the guards. When they saw her leaping through the brush, breasts bouncing in the moonlight, the guards realized what they'd interrupted. This, grumps Dirk, sent them into paroxysms of laughter.

For twenty minutes, the guards made fun of Dirk in broken English. "She run," they giggled. "Bye-bye! No sex for you." They dragged him around the circumference of the hill to watch Abby

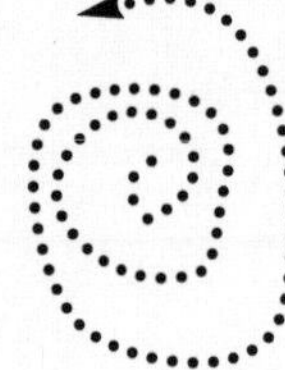

wind her way through the city, screaming with laughter every time she disappeared into the shadows.

[Abigail's route]

*

TRACY IS A PROFESSIONAL FITNESS INSTRUCTOR. We're talking hard-core hard body. She's got the personality to back it up, too. Her favourite verbs are *punch* and *pump*. She mixes raw eggs into her morning smoothies.

Every year, Tracy challenges herself with a new activity. Last year, it was rock climbing. Next year, it'll be a Strongman competition. This year, it's her PADI (Professional Association of Diving Instructors) open-water certificate.

Booking time off work, she travels to Jamaica to put in some serious PADI time. She's devoted—even though she's using her official vacation time, Tracy's up every morning at seven to jog and do yoga. She's at the beach by nine.

Her first day on the beach, a local named Jermaine takes an interest in her technique. A divemaster, Jermaine offers tips for improvement. Tracy scans his lean frame. Nice. But she's here to work.

On her second day, Jermaine waves at her underwater. They surface and talk about the diving hot spots in the area. Over the next two days, Jermaine shows up everywhere Tracy goes: poolside during downward dog position, at the bar for her evening drink, and even at the local café where Tracy eats jerk pork and ackee pie that's so good she wants to cry.

Every time, Jermaine acts surprised to see her. He's charming, and when he asks her to go diving with him, Tracy agrees. An outing with someone as experienced as Jermaine will punch up her game, she thinks.

They meet the next day at nine in the morning. On the way to his special diving spot, Jermaine points out interesting landmarks. She asks if she can steer the boat for a while and he indulges her. After half an hour, Jermaine pulls up and drops anchor. The sea is so blue and the sky so bright, Tracy feels blinded. It's a relief when they gear up and dive.

Nothing prepared her for what she sees. It's breathtaking. The deeper Jermaine takes her, the more she's convinced that heaven lies beneath the sea. At eighty feet, Tracy never wants to surface. She looks at Jermaine—she wants to signal that she loves this. She's placing her hands over her heart when she notices Jermaine struggling with his dive suit. In a moment, he's naked. Tracy is astounded. *What's he doing?*

Jermaine swims toward her. He comes closer. Tracy is confused. He swims past her face, penis brushing against her hair. *Oh. That's what he's doing.* He swims past her again. Tracy motions for him to go away. He does it again, and this time he hovers with his penis right near her face. *Gimme a break.* She pushes him. Jermaine motions for her to get undressed. Tracy gives him the finger. His eyes crinkle. *The stupid bugger is smiling. Isn't flipping the bird a universal sign?*

Jermaine swims past, fluffing his floating family jewels. *He's like a friggin' eel.* With limited ways to communicate, Tracy decides on a course of action. She motions to Jermaine to stop swimming. He watches as she points to his penis, points to herself, and shakes her finger: no. Tracy points at his penis again and then holds her thumb and forefinger an inch apart.

Jermaine's suit is soon back on. The date ends shortly thereafter.

*

JANUARY 31, 2004, 1:02 A.M.

A kitchen in downtown Toronto.

"For the first five nights that I'm in Mexico, I'm sick. I can't hang out or sightsee. It's awful," says Glenna, pouring herself another glass of Merlot. The twenty-eight-year-old strawberry blonde settles back into her chair. "Finally, on the sixth night, the day before I'm about to head further south, I feel better."

Three days earlier, Glenna got back from a two-week trip visiting friends—Robin and Grant—in Mexico. Five girlfriends pull together an impromptu cocktail party and urge Glenna to share tales of her adventures.

This one is about Jorge.

Chomping into a spring roll, Glenna chews and resumes her story. "We go out for dinner, then to this tiny little bar that Robin and Grant like," she says.

The bartender, Jorge, has become a friend. Well, he gives them free drinks and that's the main reason Robin and Grant keep going back.

Jorge is oh-my-God hot. Black hair worn in a thick braid. Dark eyes and big lips. *Ai caramba!*

At the bar, Glenna can't keep her eyes off of Jorge. They play cards, he pours free drink after free drink, and Glenna is loaded. At four in the morning, Jorge closes the bar and Robin—answering the silent plea Glenna shoots her—invites him back to the apartment.

"We go up to the patio and there's the most beautiful view in the world," sighs Glenna. "The town stretches across two small, steep mountains and we're on one side looking across a valley of tea lights. It's just gorgeous."

Robin and Grant disappear to bed. Jorge and Glenna stare at one another for an endless moment. She grabs his hand and he smiles.

"I felt like I was fifteen again," she says, her friends nodding in shared understanding.

They are communicating in a mix of Spanish, English, and French. Glenna offers a tentative "Can I kiss you?" Jorge answers, "Of course."

Five minutes later, Jorge has ripped Glenna's jeans off. "Holy shitballs," Glenna says, remembering, "he's *hot.* We look for condoms, but I don't have any."

Jorge says he's got some back at his place, which is on the other side of the valley. It's now five in the morning. It's freezing out and at least a half-hour walk, but off they go. When they reach the centre of town, people are getting up to go to work. Glenna has to catch a bus in four hours.

"Up the other side of the valley, just as we reach this bright orange building with a blue door, the sun comes up," says Glenna. "It's huge. Sunshine streaming down, warming us up. It was beautiful."

Entering his living room, Jorge flips on the light. Glenna is stunned into silence. There, crowding the four walls of his apartment, are enormous dry-mounted photographs of the rock band KISS.

As Glenna searches for something, anything, to say, Jorge whips off his shirt. His chest is an immediate distraction. Dark hair covering his pecs, flat stomach, treasure trail. He's stunning.

Then he turns around. Glenna can't believe her eyes. There, inked across his entire back, is a KISS tattoo. All four members of the band are displayed between Jorge's broad, stacked shoulders.

"You slept with him anyway, didn't you," one of Glenna's girlfriends accuses.

Glenna giggles and pours more wine. "Of course," she answers. But she made him turn off the lights first.

*

LUCA IS DETERMINED to get into Alicia's pants. At least, that's what she *thinks* he's up to. For the umpteenth time that night, Alicia wishes she'd learned a few key words of Italian before travelling around this country. The only thing she says is *poco, poco,* which means, she thinks, either "slowly" or "a little."

She met Luca yesterday. Alicia, standing in front of a building that looked like a church, was lost and trying to find the church on her map. Behind her, a man's voice said, "Vroom, vroom," into her ear. Turning, Alicia laid eyes on one of the world's most stunning creatures. Tall and lanky with chiselled features and peepers that could only be described with cheesy romance clichés like "dreamy" or "bedroom eyes."

Luca indicated that she was, in fact, staring at a car dealership. He helped her find the church. She flirted. He asked her to dinner. She accepted. They ate and misunderstood one another for three hours. It was lovely, and so he asked her to meet him again tonight.

After dinner at a sidewalk café, Luca leads Alicia down to the beach. Earlier, the hostel manager told her that "going to the beach" in Finale Ligura means "making out," and to watch herself with young Italian men. They only want one thing. Well, thinks Alicia, she only wants one thing, too, and she's pretty sure it's the same thing as Luca.

Luca gestures to Alicia to climb over a flimsy fence erected on the beach. He throws himself over it. "*Andiamo,*" he says, moving his hands in a way that reminds Alicia of training her puppy years ago. Using himself as bait is pretty smart, she muses while heaving herself over the fence onto the private beach.

"Desire destiny cedar tree?" Alicia hears, and she sees Luca pointing to a lounge chair on the beach. *Okay. Sit. I understand that. Oh. Okay. I'll sit on him. Sounds good. Maybe he's as hard as a cedar tree. Is cedar hard wood or soft?*

In one butter-smooth move, Luca pulls Alicia onto his lap

and into a kiss. *Heavens to Betsy,* thinks Alicia. *Heavens to Betsy? Where did that come from?* She starts to giggle.

That's when Luca places one long, tapered finger against her lips and says in a deep, husky whisper: "See it Malta *bella.* Volley farewell *amore* boy."

She can't see Malta, but she understands the language of love. *Bella? Amore?* Crystal clear.

Alicia dives in for another kiss and rips open his button-down shirt. Luca, obviously well versed in sign language, groans and lifts the hem of her skirt. They're all over each other. They're like animals. They're kissing, nipping, biting, groaning, moaning, and—heavens to Betsy—about to have sex.

"Stop!" screeches Alicia. *Oh shit. Condoms. How does one say* condom *in Italian?* "You. Condom?" She mimes the act of ripping open the foil and rolling a condom down.

"*Preservatiavo?* No."

They gaze at one another, hungry and sad. Panting, Luca perks up. "I straddle pretty much finger."

"What?"

"I straddle pretty much finger," repeats Luca, jumping from the chair and humping the air. As Alicia watches slack jawed, Luca jerks his hips into the air ever more violently until, pretending he's about to come, he leaps away from his invisible partner and, using his finger, mimes sperm shooting into the sand.

Oh, thank God. I don't want him straddling my finger. Blech.

Luca comes back over to the chair and waits for Alicia's response. He starts to lick her neck and, once again, she's reminded of her puppy. She melts a little under his soft tongue and then pulls herself together. *No. This can't happen. I have no idea what diseases he might have. He could have herpes or AIDS or warts or something.* Alicia tears herself away from Luca.

"No. You could have a disease. Herpesi? Warta?" She feigns coughing and points to his groin.

"Pens ate *che* hot innate *alfredo* dalmation penis?"

He doesn't understand, thinks Alicia. *I don't understand.* She hacks and sneezes and pretends to faint. "Warta. Herpese. AIDSa? *Capiche?*"

"No." He looks alarmed.

Alicia gets up from the chair and points to his groin. She mimes sperm shooting out, landing on her, and then she gags, points at him, coughs, retches, and falls down on the sand, playing dead.

"Sperm lucid era?"

"Yes. *Si.* Sperm. Sicko. Diseasa."

She waves toward him and fakes dying once more.

Luca stares at her and then gets up from the chair. He waits for Alicia to brush the sand off her ass and then walks back toward the fence. She's disappointed. She thought they could still fool around, at least, but she follows in silence.

HANDY TRAVEL VOCABULARY

ENGLISH	ITALIAN	FRENCH
AIDS	sussidi	SIDA
herpes	erpete	herpes

The next morning, when Alicia goes down to breakfast in the hostel lounge, the manager asks to speak with her. Luca, it turns out, is the son of a close friend. After dropping Alicia off, Luca was rattled and sought out a stiff drink with the manager. Between shots of tequila, Luca told the tale of their aborted tryst and explained why he was so freaked out. What he understood Alicia to say from her miming was that if a man sleeps with her, his penis falls off.

*

THEY SAY WHAT HAPPENS IN LAS VEGAS, stays in Las Vegas but, unfortunately, that doesn't always hold true. Many of us, while abroad, threw off the shackles of "respectability," "responsibility," and "reputation." We went wild. We yanked off our bras in New

York bars for free drinks and to catch the eye of the scuzzy musician in the corner. We did tequila shots out of navels on solid German bellies. We spent days lounging naked on Thailand's beaches. We went crazy, only to have the whiff of a one-night stand with François or Dieter stink up our lives once we're back home.

Years later, after I left the Lycée and moved back to Canada, I met the mother of my old upchuck chum, Peter, at a black-tie event. I'd remained friends with Pete throughout the years, so she knew who I was and sought me out. A striking woman in her fifties, Sally had the kind of elegance that inspires trust and immediately puts one at ease. For some unfortunate reason, however, Sally's presence also made me babble. "I never understood why you and Pete weren't an item," she said, after we exchanged pleasantries. "I always thought the two of you would be perfect together."

"Well, Sally," I began, my mind willing, pleading, *begging* my mouth not to go any further. It was too late. "We made out once, but then I threw up on him. And when someone pukes on you, the chemistry tends to die, but, because a mother should know this about her son, he was a perfect gentleman about it. We washed ourselves off in the sea and he never called again. Not that I wanted him to, I mean. Wait. . . ."

You have a reputation for being straight forward and honest.

Sally patted me on the shoulder. "That's good to know," she said, and kissed me goodbye on the cheek. "Take care."

Many an avaricious monster may thank
his doting parents for qualities which
render him odious.

WILLIAM WALLING, *Sexology*, 1904

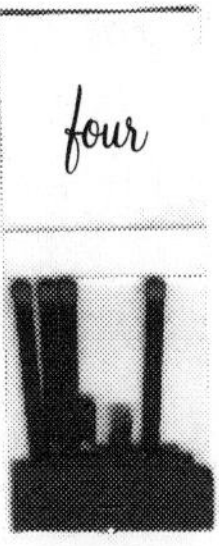

Overly Familial

FROM THE MOMENT MY sister and I moved out of my parents' home, we've been able to count on two things without fail: Dad will send money just before we run out of Ramen noodles, and Mum will call first thing in the morning after a date the night before.

During her mid-twenties, my sister lived in New York. The city was everything she'd dreamed of: a tiny, organized apartment in Hell's Kitchen with lawn chairs on the roof, the latest designer knock-offs displayed in deserted parking lots, and celebrities sipping lattes in the local café. She soaked up the city and, by twenty-six, my sister was cynical, ahead of the pack, and in her element.

My sister met Matthew through an ex-boyfriend. He was a nice guy. Nothing more. But, a believer in keeping the pheromones humming, she'd agreed to go out on a few dates with him.

One Friday night, my sister was getting ready for a date with Matthew. The phone rang. It was our mother.

"What are you doing tonight, honey?" my mother asked.

In a fit of insanity, my sister told her the truth. My mother loves nothing more than to probe her daughters' love lives. "How old is he? How did you meet? What does he do? Who are his parents? What does he look like?"

"Mum, it's nothing. No big deal. I mean, I don't even know why I'm going out with him. He's kind of boring and he's way too short. He's nice, but there are no sparks."

My sister managed to squeeze Mum off the phone, after listening to two bits of unsolicited advice: "Don't wear black like you always do" and "do wear control top pantyhose."

My sister ignored the first piece of advice but took the second one.

At eight o'clock on Saturday morning, as my sister was trying to figure out how she could remove her arm from beneath Matthew's frame without waking him up, the phone rang. She let the answering machine pick up.

"Hi, honey," our mother's voice called out in a cheery tone. "Calling to see how your big date went last night. Hope you gave him a chance. Just because he's short doesn't mean he's not Mr. Right, now does it? Now. What did you wear? Please don't say you wore something black—sweetie, colours really become you! And thank God for control top. I'm sure you're out for a run, but call me the minute you get back and we can chat about Matthew. Love you. Bye. Kiss, kiss."

My sister (who does not run) now has call display.

*

FAMILIES EMBARRASS US. That's what they do. Older brothers pull our pants down at the cottage in front of the boy we're crushing on. Younger sisters read our diaries out loud to friends for a quarter. Parents say inappropriate things in public, like "When did you start wearing thongs?" or "Would you please stop picking that zit?"

Even when they're trying hard not to make us cringe, parents, grandparents, uncles, aunts, siblings, and cousins still make unintentional faux pas. The woman whose father walks around nude in the house, for example. Well, it's his house. He can do what he likes, but it's tricky bringing home a boyfriend unannounced. The man whose mother can't help but lick her thumb and wipe away a smudge on his thirty-year-old cheek. The brother who accidentally calls a woman by her family nickname: Gassypants.

This is why, in therapy, so many issues are rooted in family. Indeed, it's become a common joke. But despite suffering intense, life-altering mortification at the hands of the people who are supposed to love us most, we survive. Somehow, we manage to find the confidence to date, even when our family baggage is cumbersome. That hundreds of thousands of us find a partner with complimentary baggage is extraordinary. You have to kiss a lot of frogs before that happens. And, like a therapist, we hear a lot of horror stories. But we date. We deal.

Spot the complimentary baggage!

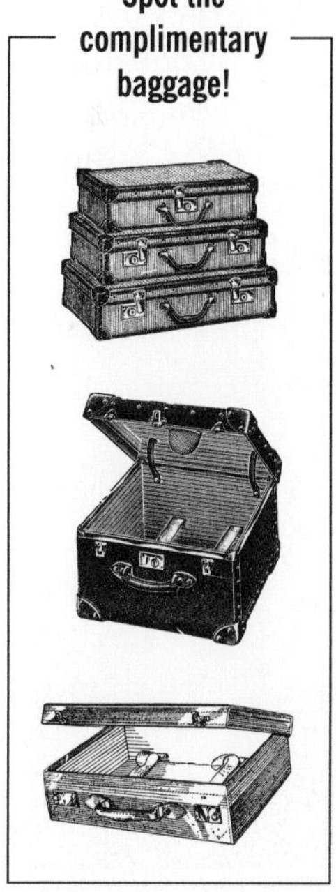

*

"MOM?"

"Honey, how was your date with Henry?"

"Why on earth did you think I'd be attracted to that guy?"

"Henry's a very nice young man. What happened?"

"He picked me up. He took me to the *fish* market."

"Well, it's creative."

"It's disgusting. Guts, gills, eyes. And it stinks."

"He's on his way up at the firm."

"He's a drip. Moping around, not asking me any questions."

"Maybe he was nervous. You're a beautiful, confident woman. That can scare a man. You can be intimidating."

Silence.

"After the fish market, where did you two go?"

"A café."

"What did you order?"

"A chocolate sundae."

"That sounds nice."

"He started to cry."

Silence.

"I asked him what was wrong. Chocolate makes him cry, Mom."

"Honey. . . ."

"Mom. Did you know that his father, who worked at the Hershey factory, had a heart attack, fell into a huge vat of chocolate, and drowned?"

"Honey, that's just awful."

"So why are you laughing?"

✻

BETH AND MORGAN ARE CO-WORKERS. Sparks are always in the air whenever they're together. Reporters for a community newspaper, they've gone out a few times (drinks after work with other people from the newsroom) and experienced one awkward night in a motel room while working on a story together (Beth was bloated with her period and there was no way she was going to fool around with him).

One afternoon, Morgan asks Beth to a movie on Saturday night. Saturday. It's as close to a date as they've gotten. Beth's heart swells. She accepts.

Saturday. Beth races to get ready. She tries on a dozen different clothing combinations: black jeans, *too tight*; red miniskirt, *might as well announce I'm a whore*; blue jeans, *he sees me in these every day*; brown cords, *hello, fat thighs.* She settles on the single woman's best friend: a simple, form-flattering black skirt. A pale blue cashmere crewneck sweater and a gorgeous black trench coat borrowed from her mother complete her outfit.

Morgan arrives and they head off to the movie. Beth can't keep her mind on the film—Morgan's firm thigh is pressed against hers. It's almost unbearable. The movie ends just in time. She was about to jump down his throat.

In the car, Morgan asks Beth if she'd like to come back to his place for tea. *Is he kidding? A single, straight man drinks tea on a Saturday night? I don't buy it,* thinks Beth, *but I'm game.* "Sure," she says.

They reach Morgan's apartment and he gives Beth a quick tour—neat, sparse, lots of CDs and books. He proceeds to brew a pot of tea. He knows what he's doing, notes Beth. He warms the cups and steeps the antique china pot. He sets out a sugar bowl, creamer, and silver spoons. They sip their tea—it's excellent—and Morgan's cat weaves into the room. He pours some cream into a china saucer and places it on the ground. *This guy is unreal,* thinks Beth.

Over three cups of tea, the flirting continues. The conversation is easy and comfortable. Tension thrums, and Beth doesn't want it to end.

Finally, Beth decides she should leave. It's one in the morning; she needs to pee and is antsy from too much caffeine. Slipping on the trench coat, Beth sends out the kiss-me vibe. *Kiss me. Kiss me. Kiiiiissss meeeeee.*

Morgan extends the conversation with inane chatter about a story he's working on. Beth lingers at the door. Neither one makes a move. Beth ups the ante. "Well, I better go," she says, reaching into her coat pocket to get car keys. She pulls them out. Morgan's eyes widen. Beth looks at her hand. Caught up in her key ring are her mother's false teeth.

Horrified, Beth shoves her hand back into the pocket. She's bright red. *Did he see them? I don't know how he could have missed them. Does he think they are mine? Oh dear God.*

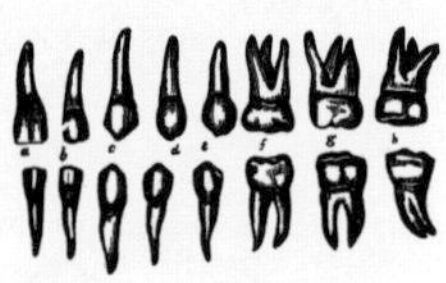

Beth pretends it didn't happen. Morgan keeps talking, but the romantic mood is gone. She's certain he keeps looking at her teeth. Feigning exhaustion, Beth runs out of his building.

Note: Morgan never asked Beth out again. Beth's mother was fitted for more comfortable false teeth, which she now never removes from her mouth unless at home. Beth doesn't borrow her mother's coats any more.

*

"HI, HON. IT'S ME."

"Hey. Where are you? I tried you at home, but got the machine."

"I'm still at work. I've got to finish crunching all of these numbers tonight."

"That's crazy, Lynn. You know they take total advantage of you, right?"

"I know, I know." *Sigh.* "What are you up to? Did I catch you in the middle of something?"

"No. Just cleaning the kitchen for Mom."

"Oh. Rob, that's exactly why, at twenty-seven, you should have your own apartment."

"But they'd be so upset. . . . We've been through this."

"I know." *Pause.* "Sorry."

"We still on for tomorrow night?"

"Yeah. A movie?"

"Sounds good."

"And some cuddling."

"Definitely."

* * *

"Hi."

"Lynn. I called you at work."

"Just got in the door. How are you?"

"Great. I got the contract."

"Rob! That's fantastic news."

"Yeah, I'm pretty pumped."

"That's great." *Pause.* "Soooo, did you ask?"

"Uh, yeah."

"And?"

"She still said no."

"That's ridiculous."

"I'll talk to her in the morning."

* * *

"Hey."

"Hey."

"What did she say?"

"Listen, Mom's just not ready to have me spend the night at your house."

"Fuck, Rob. You're an adult. And you're still a virgin. Does she know that?"

"I don't discuss sex with my parents, Lynn."

"But they want you to be a normal guy, right?"

"I know all the arguments, and I know you think it's strange, but I've got to be sure that my parents are okay with this before I sleep over. We've agreed to talk about it more tonight when I get home." *Pause.* "You do know that I'm still not ready to have sex, don't you?"

"Yes. And I respect that. But after three months of dating, it's not unusual for a girl to want her boyfriend to sleep over. Even if it is just cuddling."

* * *

"Hi Lynn. It's me. Guess what? I can sleep over tomorrow night! I talked to Mom and convinced her I wasn't going to hell if I just slept in the same bed as you. For some reason, it helped when I said you have a queen-sized bed. Whatever. If it makes her feel better, then so be it. She asked if I was still a virgin and then she asked if I was going to lose it to you. That was a pretty awkward conversation. Anyway, I'll tell you more about when I hear from you. Bye."

* * *

"Rob?"

"Yeah."

"You asleep?"

"No."

"Are you comfortable? I mean, you keep tossing."

"It's boiling in here."

"I've got the window open."

"Can you open it more?"

"No. It's open all the way." *Pause.* "Maybe you should take off your pants?"

"Lynn. I told you that I don't want to have sex. And I really don't want to have this conversation again."

"I was just thinking, *Rob*, that the reason you're so hot might be because you're wearing track pants, shorts, and boxers."

"I'm just being honest with you."

"Okay. While we're being honest, you should know that this whole 'gotta check with Mommy' thing is getting old. I want to have sex. I'm twenty-six years old. That's what twenty-six-year-old women do. And, to be perfectly honest, I'm getting to the point where I don't want to have sex with you, especially when you come to bed—for the first time, I might add—looking like the Michelin man."

Pause.

"Mom said this would be a mistake."

*

COURTNEY IS MEETING NICK'S PARENTS for the first time. She's nervous because she really likes Nick—it's been five months, and she's starting to think about moving in with him. At thirty-three, Nick's keen on "taking the next step." Dinner with his family, he says, is so she can see "where he comes from." (Nick's one annoying habit is talking in quotations.)

When they pull up in front of Nick's parents' home, Courtney is impressed. Andrea and Henry live in an adorable bungalow. Andrea is an avid gardener, and colourful flower beds line the walk. Henry, a retired contractor, has built sleek wood patio furniture and arranged it on the front porch.

"My sister, brother-in-law, and aunt will also be here," warns Nick. "I have to tell you something. My dad has a bad habit of calling any woman I bring home by the name of my last girlfriend. He thinks it keeps the women 'on edge' and on their 'best behaviour.' I'm sorry about this. I've tried talking to him about it, but he refuses to listen."

Courtney smiles and urges him not to worry. She can deal with that. What is his last girlfriend's name, by the way? Just so she knows when she's being addressed.

"It's Gloria," says Nick.

Nick's family greets them the minute they enter the house. It isn't until they're settled in the living room that Henry pulls his old trick.

"What can I get you to drink, Gloria?"

"A gin and tonic, thanks," says Courtney.

Over the next forty-five minutes, Henry uses *Gloria* eight times. Each time, Courtney responds without comment. Each time, Nick corrects his father. His mother and sister roll their eyes and offer apologetic looks.

At dinner, the conversation turns to Courtney's work in child care.

"So tell me, Gloria, what ages do you work with?" asks Henry.

"It's Courtney, Dad. Please. You know that," interrupts Nick.

Courtney, fine with ignoring the insulting antics of Nick's father, is suddenly incensed that Henry would put Nick through this embarrassing display.

"No, no, it's fine," says Courtney, turning to Nick's father. "I completely understand, Horace."

You will be sought out for your diplomatic skills, Lucky Numbers 3, 7, 22, 24, 27, 33

Henry, biting into some steamed cauliflower, chokes. A shocked silence descends on the table. Every head swivels to stare at him. Courtney, who thought her comment might ease the tension and make the family laugh, is surprised by the reaction of the room. Henry clears his throat and turns to Nick. "So, what've you been up to lately?"

The next forty-five minutes are utter hell. Nick's mother smiles stiff lipped at Courtney, and Nick's sister stares at her with open disapproval. The brother-in-law chats with Courtney until his wife interrupts them to ask his opinion on the new china set on the sideboard. Nick's aunt, Henry's sister, keeps winking at her and stifling giggles with her napkin. Otherwise, the "misnamer" is completely ignored.

The one time that Henry is forced to interact with Courtney, she notices he uses her proper name. Nick tries in vain to keep Courtney in the conversation.

"What happened in there?" asks Courtney as soon as they escape. "Was that rude?"

"No. Not at all," says Nick, starting the car. "He deserved it. He was being a jerk. I'm so sorry about this. It's just that you called him *Horace*. Why did you pick that name?"

"I don't know. Sounds like Henry, I guess. Why?"

Horace, it turns out, is the name of Henry's estranged twin brother. Growing up, the two were confused for one another all the time. No one in the family can remember what their initial argument was about, but the twins haven't spoken in twenty years. Any time someone says the name *Horace*, Nick explains to Courtney, his father's immediate reaction is to mutter, "Jackass."

> **Henry:** from the Germanic name Heimerich, meaning lord of the manor, estate ruler
>
> **Horace:** Latin clan name meaning ~~timekeeper~~ jackass

*

LESLIE AND ED FALL IN LOVE eight days before Christmas. Within five minutes of meeting each other, they're smitten. They spend the next seven days shopping together, eating together, and sleeping together. The only time they're apart is when they have family obligations. They have a touching, sweet conversation in which they agree that both feel it's too soon to introduce each other to family. Further proof that they're meant to be.

The night before Christmas, Leslie gives in. Her mom's on her back about meeting Ed, and her dad is threatening to call him just so her mom will stop harping on the subject.

With grave misgivings, Leslie invites Ed to a dinner party at her parents' home. The house is a zoo. Leslie is one of five children (ages range from Leslie, the oldest at twenty-seven, to Morissey, the youngest at eleven), and at the house that night are also two aunts, two uncles, a grandmother, and the neighbours. When the door to the house opens, a cacophony of family bickering, laughing, teasing, and story sharing assaults them. Ed, who comes from a family of three, looks uneasy but is soon pitching in with dinner and playing with Mo.

After dinner, as various family members clutch bellies and moan on sofas, Leslie's father announces that this year, unlike any other, they will be going to church for midnight service. The family is stunned. They are most definitely not church types. When Mo asks what religion they are, it takes Leslie a moment to remember.

Ed, however, has been to church often, and Leslie is eager to impress him.

At the church, they find a place to sit—all sixteen of them squeezed into two pews. At the far end of one pew, Ed is sandwiched between Leslie and Mo, who's taken a shine to this new friend of his sister's.

The choir sings. The readings are read. And then the minister gets up to deliver the sermon. The church is silent. He opens his mouth and . . . *PFFFFFFT!* An ear-splitting fart echoes through the church. Leslie turns to stare at Ed. He's bright red.

The minister tries to recover and starts speaking. Leslie looks at her date, wide eyed. Ed, shaking his head, points a thumb at Mo, who is giggling like a madman in his seat. As

Leslie watches, Mo raises one leg and waits for another pause in the sermon.

"Mo," hisses Leslie. "No."

Too late. Another fart bounces off the stained glass windows. People start to giggle. Others turn sharply and stare at Ed. His pale, freckled skin is now the colour of a fire engine.

"Dad," Leslie taps her father in the pew in front of them. "Get Mo to stop! Please!" She's frantic. Mo's lifting his leg again.

When he turns around, Leslie's father has tears running down his cheeks. She's confused until she realizes that he's laughing. "Dad. For God's sake, pull yourself together. We're in church." This sets her father off again.

Leslie tries to get her mother's attention at the far end of the pew, but her mom is pretending that she doesn't know them. Feigning a look of disgust, her mother rolls her eyes at other people in the church. Leslie waves her arms at her mother and, just then, with Leslie half out of her seat, another fart rips through the air.

Ed is purple with embarrassment. Leslie is ready to throttle her little brother. Her grandmother's stiff and powdered friends are apoplectic. The minister is staring at their pew. Her so-called family is either stifling laughter or pretending that they're unrelated. Leslie could just die.

Mo farts two more times before he runs out of, ahem, gas. When safely out of the church and away from people's stares, Ed assures Leslie he's fine and bids her goodnight.

Should have trusted my instincts, moans Leslie. *It was way too soon to introduce him to my family.*

❋

"FRITZ? IS THAT YOU? Oh my heavens, is this beautiful girl your little friend? Jillian? Oh, aren't you just gorgeous! I knew you would be. Fritz is very picky about pretty things. I just love your hair and that dress. You must tell me where you buy such a thing. I'm Hedda, Fritz's mama. Now don't you go calling me Mrs. I'll be very upset with you. What? You've brought me a gift! Fritz, darling, don't let this girl get away. What manners. And she's too good looking; you'll lose her for sure. You know, Jillian, we always thought Fritz was a little, what's the phrase? Light feet. He has light feet, that's it. But no! Such relief when he starts talking about the girl he met at the bar. 'Oh, Mama, her name's Jillian and she's so smart!' The gushy talk. You get to my age, you don't use it so much. But what a relief for his poor mama. I was so worried. Oh, Fritz, don't get your shorts bunched up. Jillian's almost family, isn't she? And better your mother tell her our worries than that big mouth, Ida. My sister doesn't ever stop. Chatter, chatter, chatter. Like a bird. What are those little cheepers called? Not parrots, you silly boy. Those brown ones. Doesn't matter. She's a talker. Now, Jillian, I want to show you baby pictures of Fritz. Even then he was nice and big, if you know what I mean. What's that saying about horses, Fritz? Or donkeys? Why are you red? We're two women talking woman talk. Now, I don't want to know because I'm his mother, but if my memory is good—and his father is not so great—but if my memory is right, you're happy in bed. Fritz, you are such a baby. 'Mama!' Like you're ashamed of me. Stop. We're adults. Jillian, could you take this lemonade out to the sundeck? I thought we'd sit out there, it's such a sunny day and . . . oh, no, darling. You can't push the glass door from the middle. You must use the side of the door. The metal part. Fritz, get the Windex. Jillian, I like a clean house. Thank you for the 'I'm sorry's but you must understand—you're going to be around for a while, right, Fritz? I hope so. Fritz with a girl is such a blessing. But you must know that if you put your hand on glass and leave a print, like you just did, that's not my house. You must clean it. Here, I'll take the lemonade. I want to show you where I keep the Windex and wipes. I'll show you how to clean it properly. What? Fritz! You want I should keep a dirty smudge on my window?"

Though Jillian is no longer in contact with Fritz, she has heard through the grapevine that he is working as a hairdresser and living with a lovely man named David. Fritz's mother is devastated.

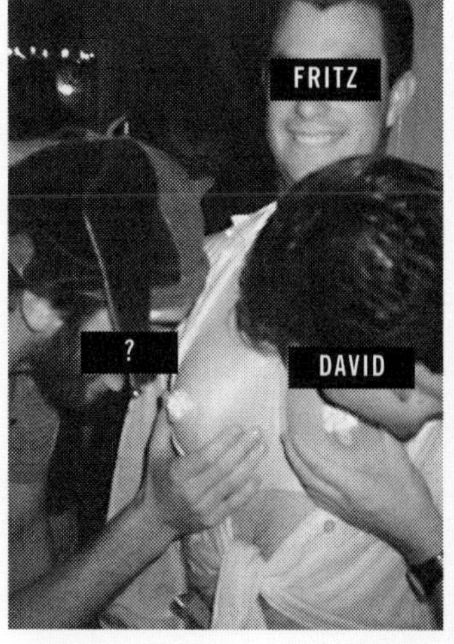

"This young man has never been at Paris."
A sigh sometimes followed this silent ejaculation.

ANN RADCLIFFE, *The Mysteries of Udolpho,* 1794

Credentials

WHEN I MEET HARRY, I'm twenty-five years old, single, and prone to self-delusion. He's forty-four (only nineteen years difference—no biggie, right?). He's separated with one child (I love children! I'd be a great stepmom!). Playing a gig at the local hotel, Harry sings slightly off-key, crooning about heartache and pain. I have a glass of cheap white wine.

The music is bland. Harry, however, is yummy. Tall, lean, and handsome in that older movie star way—think Richard Gere in *Pretty Woman*. During the band's break, he notices me. We smile. He asks for my phone number. I oblige and then leave before I'm stuck listening to his second set.

A few days later, Harry calls me.

"Would you like to go to a movie?"

"Love to."

"It has to be an early one, 'cause my sitter can't stay past eleven." Harry's willing to get a sitter in order to go on a date with me—oh, warm fuzzies.

He picks me up at 6:30 p.m. The first comment from his mouth is about the largeness of my cat. He looks at her like she's a wildebeest. Annoyed, I somehow manage to refrain from remarking on his tasselled loafers.

During the drive to the theatre, the only thing he asks me about is my age. "Ah," is his reply.

I ask him about his son, his music, his house, and his hobbies. He answers in monosyllables. I wonder why on earth he asked me out.

During the movie, we sit together like two strangers who happen to be sharing popcorn. After the movie, we talk about the plot. This takes five minutes.

Harry drives me home. I'm exhausted from trying so hard to make conversation. Finally, in a last-ditch effort to salvage the evening, I babble. "So, you've managed to make a career in music? That's amazing. Do you only play local bars? I've heard it's really difficult to break into larger markets but, you know, if you're talented then—"

"Well," he interrupts, "I have a day job."

A tidbit of information. I pounce.

"What do you do?"

"I'd rather not say."

"C'mon, I won't tell."

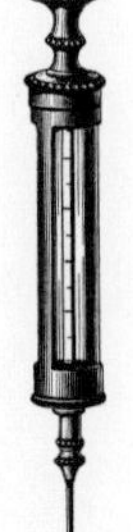

"I work at a hospital."

"And . . . ?"

"I'm an anaesthetist. I put people to sleep."

I'll say. I couldn't stand it any longer. "Right. Well, 'night. Thanks for the movie."

"You're welcome. Listen, can you not tell people that I'm an anaesthetist? I don't want to be known as the musician who puts people to sleep."

"Right. Gotcha."

We never spoke again.

[TEDIUM TONIC]

*

IT'S HAMMERED INTO US, from an early age, that education is important. It starts out with reading, writing, and adding apples. School's fun. But before we know it, our courses have morphed into a fiendish brew of calculus, chemistry, and civics. "You want to work at Burger King?" Meant to be a threat, of course, but to the young mind it sounds pretty good. Free burgers and fries. Cool.

While we're still thinking about our first kiss, we're urged to get excellent grades in order to get into college or university. The implication is that only with a degree, especially from a "good" school, will we be able to get the jobs we want. How do we know what job we want when we haven't ever stayed out past ten o'clock?

This cycle never ends. Train, learn, improve, work harder, work longer, strive, push, beat the rest. It's easy to get sucked in and then wake up one morning and wonder where the laughter has gone.

If you're smart and have plenty of confidence, you can reject this high-speed, take-no-prisoners approach. Even if you thrive in that environment, you'll be emotionally healthy as long as you keep your life in balance.

It's when people let the pressure eat away at their souls that it becomes a problem. With half our waking life spent at work/school or thinking about work/school, it's no wonder we develop neuroses based on work and education. The trick is learning to cope with these issues while on a date.

*

BACK IN THE MID-1990S, before Internet dating became an acceptable way to meet someone, Naomi had a girlfriend named Sue who fancied herself a matchmaker. Sue placed an ad in the personal section of the national newspaper (to attract a higher calibre of man, or so the theory went) and would interview men over the phone. She then put them in contact with her network of girlfriends—much like on the TV show *Matchmaker*. That's how Naomi met Peter.

On the surface, Peter was everything an aspiring businesswoman could want—handsome, a self-starter with his own company, and interested in taking things slow. Sue said that he really wanted to "get to know what made a woman tick." Peter was in executive time management.

On their first date, Naomi met Peter at a diner in a trendy part of the city. Sure enough, her first impressions were very good. He was energized. He was handsome.

But then they ordered brunch.

"We would like the French toast," said Peter. Naomi thought this was rather forward. She assumed he was ordering for her (*some* guys have a sense of etiquette that defies modern times, Naomi mused), but then Peter looked at her. "What would Naomi like?"

Taken aback, and given the confusion, she also ordered the French toast.

That done, the two talked about classic first-date subjects—likes, dislikes, ambitions, family—trying to find common ground. It wasn't long before Naomi noticed Peter's peculiar verbal tic.

"A friend asked us to join his Ultimate team a year ago and we have to say that it's the best thing we ever did," Peter said, as Naomi's mind raced.

Who is he talking about? Is he married? No. Wait. No. The royal 'we'? He's talking in plural. Do I call him on it? Is this guy for real?

It was only when Peter said, "We really love bacon," with grease pooling in the corner of his mouth that Naomi couldn't stand it any longer.

"What are you doing?" she asked. "Why do you keep using 'we' and 'us'?"

"In order to be big," said Peter, unperturbed, "you have to think big."

He spoke about his team (of one) and explained that sounding as though he has more players behind him gives his conversation a certain confidence. "We tend to do this, we think like this, we agree on that. . . ."

"How am I supposed to get to know the 'team'?" asked Naomi. "Can I call them Team Member One, Team Member Two, Team Member Three?"

Wanting to have a bit of fun, Naomi started to ask questions of the different team members: "Would Bachelor Number One rather dance or dine?" "Would Bachelor Number Two pass me the sugar?"

After Naomi asked her third question ("Which bachelor chooses the music?"), the bill arrived. Peter decided it was best to split it. "That's unfair," said Naomi, a smile tugging at her lips. "You're splitting the bill with three people, and I am but one." But Peter began arguing her math. When he began to calculate the value of his time spent with her, she'd had enough. Slapping $10 on the table, Naomi grabbed her jacket and walked out.

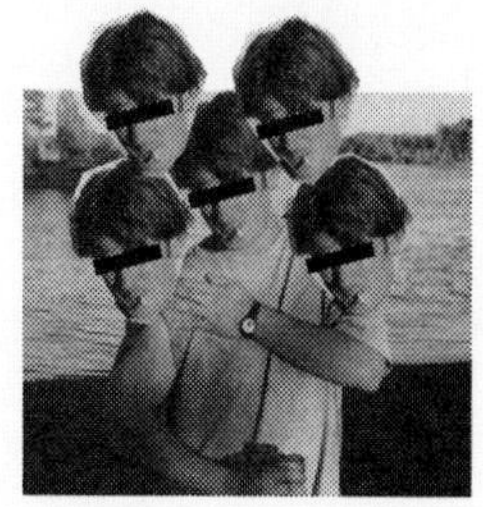

To her amazement, Peter followed. "It's important to us that we have closure," he said, looking into her eyes. "Closure, for us, means a kiss and a hug goodbye." Peter held out his arms to Naomi.

"No," stated Naomi. "My mother wouldn't approve of me kissing three people on the same date."

❋

IT WAS SPRING in Cassie's final year of high school. Every morning was filled with promise as the buds on trees hinted of hot summer nights and of the potential for romance blooming between her and Nicholas. He was a shy boy, but so sweet. They'd met at the beginning of the school year—he was in her art class. He hadn't gotten up the nerve to ask her out, but they'd shared every detail of their lives. She knew it was only a matter of time.

Cassie waited for Nicholas at their corner. Every morning, they walked to school together. "Hi, Cassie," he said, with a faint lisp that melted her heart every time. She turned and there he was. Sigh. He's adorable, thought Cassie.

At school, as she was walking down the hall to her locker, Nicholas handed Cassie a note. "Read it later," he muttered and then took off. Cassie tore it open.

Dear Kathy,
I wrot this for you.

A Harpe of Love
Loves sweat melody is playing all around
it turns eyes alit and hearts around
to make things better again.

Some loose the harpe
some just forget how to play
but love will always come back
to those whore willing to try

He got my fucking name wrong, thought Cassie. *And he can't spell.*

That summer, it rained.

*

THERE'S NOTHING JOANNA loves more in a man than long hair, a washboard stomach, and a cool job. At twenty-seven, she's not expecting to meet her future husband and so doesn't dwell too much on her rather shallow criteria. Life's too short. Love the one you're with. A girl just wants to have fun.

She meets Andy at an art opening. He's got long, slightly greasy black hair. Perfect. She falls for him when he announces that he's an artist. When he calls the opening a vernissage, she nearly loses her pants. Ooh la la.

Turns out the artist who's showing her work that night is a close friend of both Joanna and Andy. They make out behind an enormous installation piece that looks, in Joanna's humble opinion, like a giant rotten banana.

Andy calls her two weeks later, well past Joanna's deadline. He drawls an apology—"Was busy working on a show I got"—and she forgives him. "Whatcha doing later?" he asks. Joanna has plans with a girlfriend, but knows, even as she hems and haws, that those plans are toast. "I wanna see you naked," says Andy. "I think you'd be hot to paint." That's all she needs. She cancels with her girlfriend and gets naked.

Over the next three months, Joanna and Andy become a "sort of, maybe, well, we're not monogamous" item. They enjoy wild sex (Andy has the washboard abs, though Joanna suspects that's more due to his diet of cigarettes and Pop Tarts than any sort of exercise). They talk about The Dichotomy and The Iconography. They argue about her work in public relations ("shallow, corporate bullshit," says Andy). They order in Chinese food and paint each other's bodies with the soy sauce.

Every once in a while, Joanna asks to see some of his work. Andy refuses.

"I'm not ready, babe."

"It's got to be innocent. I can't have anyone critique it yet."

"I'm feeling vulnerable with this one painting. Gimme a week."

Four months into their relationship, Andy tells Joanna he's ready to show her his latest oeuvre. She's pumped. They've talked about the pieces in the abstract so often that she thinks viewing them will be like reuniting with an old friend.

She goes to his studio. It's dark. In shadow, Joanna can just make out massive canvases hanging from every wall. Paintings cover every bare surface. The smell of oil and turpentine are overwhelming (and incredibly sexy, she thinks). Andy asks her if she's ready. "Yup," she says and he flicks on the overhead fluorescent light.

Unicorns and monsters surround her. Fair blond maidens with enormous breasts holding swords across their genitalia. Birds plucking at nipples. Women in ecstasy. Women in pain. Art better suited to black velvet and the back rooms of greasy gas stations.

Words fail her. Andy misreads Joanna's silence and is pleased.

Three days later, Joanna takes a gamble. She tells Andy that she wants to take things to the next level. To her great relief, Andy breaks up with her.

*

FROM: Jen
DATE: Friday, May 14, 2004 7:14PM
TO: Amy
SUBJECT: Baby Duck

I met Dan at one of my very occasional visits to the university gym. He was cute—shaved head, big but not an inch of fat on him, pale green eyes, and about six inches taller than me. I was straddling a bilateral lat pull-down backwards when he approached; he helped me with some of the more baffling weight machines.

Dan followed me around the gym during my workout and, while I was stretching, asked me out to dinner. I hadn't gone on a date in four months, so I accepted.

Two days before our date, he called to say he was a little short on money that week and could he make me dinner instead? No problem—we were both students, so I could relate.

The day before our date, he called and asked if he could cook at my place because his was a mess. I was less happy about this, but said yes. I was young and stupid and he was very cute.

On date night, Dan turned up bearing an Old El Paso taco kit and a bottle of $9 Baby Duck from the local corner store.

With great flourish and a big mess, he cooked up the tacos. "'The will to win is important, but the will to prepare is vital,'" he quoted.

The tacos were revolting.

He drank the entire bottle of Baby Duck. "'The deepest rivers flow with the least sound,'" he announced. Then he spent two hours telling me about his love for martial arts.

He was quoting "'To fight like a warrior, you must think like a warrior,'" when my roommate came home and we acted out our code. She mimed, "Do you want me to leave?" and I signed back, "Dear God, no! Don't abandon me. Don't ever leave."

As a result, I was not the only "lucky duck" who got to see his martial arts demonstration in the middle of our living room—in which he kicked off the arm of our couch and then fell to the floor, clutching his foot in agony.

No second date.

*

OUT OF THE CARBON-COPY, university-frat-boy bunch at the Razzle Dazzle nightclub, Natalie thought she'd chosen well. Tim was very tall, very good looking, and very (as it turned out) dumb. They danced several times and made flirty small talk. At the end of the evening, he asked for Natalie's number.

When, a few days later, he invited her to his apartment for dinner, Natalie was pretty pleased.

"I knew he wasn't Nobel prize material or anything," Natalie complains to her friend Sophie. "I mean, when I was talking about my trip to Greece, he actually asked me a question about 'Lesbosians.'"

Sophie giggles. "Even the stupid ones say *lesbian* any chance they get."

"Anyway, we start making out and things are getting pretty hot. We're naked, on his bed, and he's doing all the right things. I'm on my stomach and he's on top of me. 'What do you want me to do for you?' he whispers into my ear."

"He asked you? He actually asked you what you want in bed? Keep him! Don't let a little mental inferiority stand in your way," urges Sophie.

"Wait," says Natalie. "I can't believe I'm telling you this but—promise me you won't laugh."

"Promise."

"I say, 'Kiss me all the way down to my tailbone.'"

Sophie hoots and then claps a hand over her mouth.

"You promised."

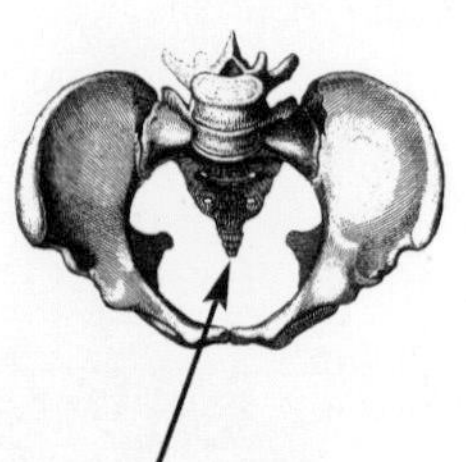

this is your tailbone

"I didn't know," Sophie says as she wipes tears from her eyes, "that you were going to say 'Kiss me down to my tailbone.'"

"Shut up. Shut up. Listen, after I say it, he answers, 'Uh, where's that?' I couldn't believe it. Some dumb, I can handle. But that dumb. . . .

"The lights came on and so did the clothes. I was out of there within ten minutes."

✻

SUNDAY, 2:30 A.M.

anecdote—*n. a short account of an entertaining or interesting incident.*

antidote—*n. a medicine, etc., taken or given to counteract poison.*

Tonight, Pat and I met up with a bunch of his friends at the bar. Even though we've been dating for the last four months, we haven't really hung out with them much, and Pat wants me to get to know his friends better. We're into our third beer when Pat starts telling a story. And then another one. He does this when tipsy—monopolizes the conversation with his "antidotes." As other people are chatting, he keeps interrupting with "That reminds me of a little antidote. . . ."

When, for a brief moment, the attention is not focused on Pat, I lean over and whisper, as I've done on other occasions, "You're mixing it up, again. It's *anecdote* not *antidote*."

He wipes beer scum from his mouth and says in a loud voice, "No, I'm not. You're wrong. I haven't wanted to say anything to you about it, but I'm tired of you correcting me."

My jaw drops.

Then I do what any self-respecting woman would do and turn to his friends and ask them: "Which is it, guys?"

They all agree with Pat! I'm done with this guy. I don't care if he does have two university degrees, I am *not* going to date a man—let alone marry a guy—who will tell our children the little *antidote* about how Mummy and Daddy got together.

Bitten by a poisonous snake? No problem.
Have we got an anecdote for you!

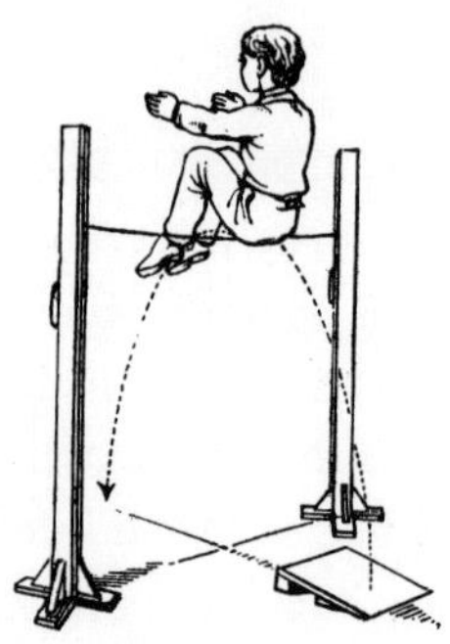

Your man needs to feel important, loved and accepted. If you won't accept his idiosyncrasies, who will? A Total Woman caters to her man's special quirks, whether it be in salads, sex, or sports.

MARABEL MORGAN, *The Total Woman*, 1973

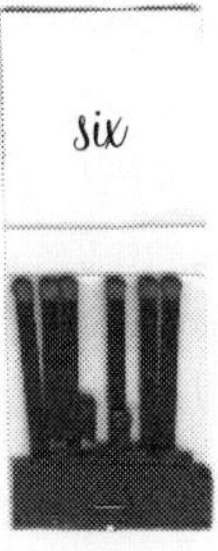

Tie Talk

"I'VE BROUGHT YOU a *longan,*" says Jason, as I climb into the passenger seat of his enormous, midnight-black Jeep Grand Cherokee. Handing over a small, brown fruit similar in size to a kiwi, my date fishes around in his jacket pocket for a jackknife. "Ever had one?" No. "You peel off the skin, like this," he shows me. "It sort of tastes like lychee." I follow his example and suck on the milk-coloured meat of the fruit. It's delicious. And sticky, very sticky. I suck the juice from my fingers and Jason leers. "I like it when you do that."

In spite of the originality of fruit on a first date, I'm already pissed at Jason. When he picked me up for the movie, he leaned on his horn rather than getting off his ass to ring the doorbell. That left me racing around like a madwoman trying to get my purse, put on boots, and find my keys while his horn blared outside, annoying my neighbours.

The movie theatre is a quick fifteen-minute ride. Jason turns it into a half-hour trek when he stops for food on the way.

"Aren't we going to get something at the movie?" I ask.

"Yeah. But I'm hungry now." He stops in Chinatown for a pork bun. He doesn't offer to get me one. He stops his car mid-lane, blocking traffic. He clambers out. "I'll be a sec."

Cars honk behind me. Sitting in this monstrous beast, I look for keys to move the car. Jason hasn't left them. I shrug at people through the window.

Honk if your date sucks

So far, this date is all about honking. I'm stressed out.

Jason returns ten minutes later. We're almost at the theatre when I notice, for the fifth time, that Jason is ogling other women while driving. "What are you doing?" I ask, as he drools over a curvy babe in a short skirt and knee-high boots.

"What?" he says.

"You know what. You're ogling women."

"So?"

"Don't you think that's offensive to the woman that you are actually on a date with?"

"What are you talking about? I'm with you, not them. Just because I look at beautiful women doesn't mean I don't think you're hot, too. I wouldn't be on a date with you if you weren't hot. I'm just appreciating them."

We arrive late. We've missed the early movie. We choose another film that starts in an hour and decide to kill time next door, browsing at the bookstore. We wander through the aisles. Both avid readers, we have a great conversation about different books we've read. He's suggesting one on war when he sees someone he knows.

"Yo, TJ," he says, slamming his knuckles against TJ's in a solid brotherhood kind of way. Without introducing me, he leads TJ off to a corner and starts talking about something. There's a creepy drug deal feel about their conversation and

I'm uncomfortable. I pick up a book on feminist theory and flip through the pages. I'm hoping for advice to get through this date.

"What's that knuckle thing about?" I ask Jason when he returns.

"I don't shake hands."

"What? Never?"

"No. You don't know where people's fucking hands have been. Guys are worse than girls. But even you were sucking on your fingers before and you haven't washed your hands since. What if you had a cold?"

"Are you serious? You were all hot and bothered over me sucking my fingers."

"Yeah. *Watching* you suck them. Doesn't mean I want to shake your hand."

*

THERE IT IS. The X factor. Who would think to worry about whether your date ogles women or suffers a form of bacillophobia? Sure, we all have quirks. Strange little emotional tics that seize us from time to time.

I, for one, refuse to share popcorn at a movie. Memories of my older sister stealing my popcorn as a child and the bald fact that every man eats popcorn like it might disappear if they don't shove it into their mouths as fast as possible, have turned me into an ogre when it comes to sharing it. I also have a thing about my fingernails, but I digress.

What I'm trying to say is that everyone has a weird thing. They may hate the colour brown, for example, or find certain birds repulsive. A friend of mine can't have anyone touch her wrists. Touch another buddy's head and he'll deck you. Most people,

Do you think I'm sexy?

however, have learned how and when to reveal this eccentricity to a love interest.

Unfortunately, some peculiarities only blossom when under stress.

❋

IT'S JUST DINNER, Freda reminds herself yet again. *Just dinner. I have dinner every day. This won't be any different. Except that it will be with another person. Paul. Oh, Paul. What if he finds me dull? No. Stop it. I am fantastic. I am woman. I am. . . . Shit. Who am I?*

Trying to remember the entire affirmation from a book her aunt gave her on womyn power, Freda struggles to pull on pantyhose. She's shy and awkward around men. None of her friends understands it. To be honest, she doesn't understand it herself. Once Freda gets to know someone, she's chatty and funny. But put her face to face with a man she's interested in and Freda chokes. The only solution she's found is drinking wine.

For some reason, Paul puts her at ease. They share mutual friends and so she's seen him a number of times at parties. In fact, Freda's best friend, Margaret, is dating Paul's best friend, George. Maybe it's that connection that makes it more comfortable for Freda. So far, she's been okay with him. At least she doesn't blush as much and she manages to answer his questions, if only with one word. This doesn't seem to put him off. Every time he sees her, it's like he's sought her out. And the last party they were at, he asked her out on a date to a romantic Cuban restaurant.

Freda would've preferred a movie.

She yanks on her pantyhose, creating a run in

the toe that she doesn't have time to deal with. *Damn.* She pours herself another quick hit of wine. She puts blush on her cheeks and cleavage and then dabs perfume between her breasts. This makes her giggle.

The doorbell rings. *I am womyn. I am hyperventilating.*

An hour later, seated in a cozy nook of the restaurant, Freda assesses the date. *Not bad. Doing okay.* Paul's interested in her artwork and is very good at drawing her out of her shell. She feels almost comfortable. *That may be the wine,* she admits, so she keeps ordering more.

They talk for two hours. The food is delicious and Freda's happy. She's not drunk. Tipsy, sure. But she's not slurring her words or anything unladylike. She's so much of a lady, in fact, that when the bill arrives, Freda doesn't even think to offer any money. She sips the last of the wine and Paul suggests that he walk her home. She agrees and struggles with her coat. He puts down money and they leave.

At her door, Paul kisses her. He places a hand on the small of her back and Freda feels faint. *It's just so simple,* thinks Freda, forgetting her history of awkward dates. He asks if he can call her. She nods, mute and mad for him. He says good night and she enters her home. *I am woman. He is man. We kiss. Just like that,* she sighs. *It's easy.*

That night, she falls into a deep, dreamless sleep.

"'I go out walking, da da dee dee, da da da da da,'" Freda hums the old Patsy Cline classic the next afternoon while dumping mouldy food from her fridge. When the phone rings, her heart leaps.

A phone call could make your heart sing.

"How much did you have to drink last night?" Freda's friend Margaret is to the point.

"I don't know. A fair bit," says Freda. "Why?"

"Paul had to go back to the restaurant this morning and apologize."

"What!?"

In the way of small social circles, George had called Paul that morning to get the scoop on how the date went. When Paul answered, explains Margaret, he was on his way back to the restaurant.

Freda is beginning to feel ill.

Apparently, continues Margaret, Paul hadn't counted on paying for so much alcohol and didn't have enough to cover the bill. Not wanting to embarrass Freda, he put down what he had and hustled her out of the restaurant. Paul returned early in the morning to pay the difference and explain to the staff why he'd stiffed them the night before.

He's never going to call me again. He must think I'm a lush.

Happily, two days later, Paul does ask Freda out again. She insists on paying.

*

FROM: Tina
DATE: Wednesday, May 12, 2004 8:00PM
TO: Amy
SUBJECT: Bad date

Several years ago, I had a date with a very attractive man. I'd met him through a friend—at her engagement party—and we got along immediately. We had similar interests and were from similar backgrounds. He called the next day to ask me to dinner.

The restaurant he chose was lovely. Delicious food, perfect ambience, classical music, and little candles. It had the makings of an excellent date until he started raging about his ex-girlfriend.

He started with "she was a bitch." In the next ten minutes, I learned that the sex was awful, she was a slob, he hated her friends, and she was a "conniving witch who only wanted to get a rock on her finger."

As the evening progressed, his anger toward his ex, and women in general, was so strong that I felt I needed to make a hasty retreat. I offered to pay for my share of the meal (I make it a point to pay my own way while I'm getting to know someone, especially on a first date).

"If you pay, that means I'll never see you again, doesn't it?" he demanded. I tried to explain to him why I'd offered to split the bill, but he was convinced that it was a brush-off.

"Are we going to see each other again?" he asked. "When? When are you free?"

"I'm going to have to think about it," I said. "I'll let you know. I have your phone number."

"No. I want to know now. Are you going to call? Why are you leaving so early? You're not going to call me, are you?"

BRASS TAPS
PIZZA PUB
682-9912
i'm the best you'll
* ever get!
PLEASE
PAY SERVER
11-17-2003 23:06 107
REG 0001 MARIA
CHECK No2

IMP.PINT	$5.05
BAR SHOT	$3.85
PIZZA 2	$6.15
SML WINGS	$5.95
7% GST	$1.47
FOOD TAX	$0.97
LIQ.TAX	$0.89
TOTAL	$24.33

He kept pushing me to find out if and when we'd go out again. I was getting fed up with his antics and so put on my coat and threw money on the table.

"I've really got to go," I said. "Take care."

"Wait. Tina," he said as I was walking out. "Wait. Don't go yet. I have to tell you something. It's important. Stop."

Intrigued by his urgency, I returned to the table.

"What?"

"I want you to know something," he said, an aggressive tone creeping into his voice. "You need to know this. It's important, so listen closely. I'm the best you'll ever get.

The. Best. You'll. Ever. Get. You should be glad that I'm even interested in you."

⁂

ANNA, TWENTY-FIVE, has just graduated from university with an engineering degree. While looking for work in her field, she's managing her uncle's restaurant, a job she held throughout her last four years of schooling. Clifford, also twenty-five, sells computer software by day. By night, however, he designs personal Web sites—a passion he hopes to turn into a career.

They meet at a wedding. Clifford is one of the few sober people there—his parents are also attending and he doesn't want to drink in front of them. Anna, who has to work early the next day, is sipping sparkling water. Clifford, ordering another Coca-Cola, notices Anna and dubs them the "Teetotaller Twins." Anna laughs. Moments later, when Clifford corrects someone who calls him "Cliff," Anna's intrigued—a man who is firm but polite, funny but not obnoxious.

Standing at the bar, they talk for a long while and discover that they're both very driven. Though Anna won't admit it out loud, she finds Clifford slightly uptight. This is, however, offset by his admiring glances. He makes her feel pretty and, when she finally squeezes a real laugh out of him, Anna suspects he might be as into her as she is him. Not the most auspicious beginning, but Anna doesn't expect earthquakes.

Over the next month, they see each other once a week. Dinner. A quick coffee after work. A walk in the park. Anna wants to get to know Clifford better and suggests a loud, smoky pub near her home. A bit of liquor in him in a place that requires him to shout, Anna thinks, and she'll crack Clifford's veneer.

It appears to be working. Not only have they played pool with some of the pub's other, more frightening, patrons, now

Clifford is urging her to play darts. "I used to play this all the time as a kid," he shouts across the room. Anna smiles. She loves darts.

She's developed a system. Before every shot, she focuses on the oche, the line on the floor behind which the players stand. She lets her eye travel along the line while turning the dart in her fingers to find a comfortable position. Then, slow and calm, she looks up to the board and shoots.

Clifford, it turns out, is an ineffective but enthusiastic player. "All right!" He pumps the air when one of his darts actually sticks to the board. "Woo hoo!"

When, after playing for thirty minutes, one of his darts hits the triple-points ring, he's exuberant. "Let's see what you can do with that," he says to Anna. She finds this side of Clifford hilarious, so she's indulging him in his boisterous behaviour. Besides, she loves a challenge.

Anna steps up to the oche. She starts to focus. Noises fade away. She finds a comfortable position. Her eyes skim along the line and, just as she looks up, Anna hears her once prim date scream, "C'mon, you fat tart! Throw the damn thing!"

Perhaps she prefers the strong, silent type after all.

*

"NINA? IT'S JEN."

"Hey. How are you?"

"Great thanks. Did Michael call?"

"Yup. He seems nice."

The two women are new friends. They met at a Valentine's Day card-making workshop a few months ago. They'd each signed up for the course while still in relationships. Both are now single.

The last time they met for drinks, Jen insisted that Nina go out with a friend of hers. Michael.

"He's wonderful," she gushed. "He's your type. And really funny, too. He wanted to take stand-up comedy classes, but didn't have enough time with his work. He's an architect."

In spite of the comedy class thing, Nina agreed to go out with him.

"So you talked? Excellent. And you thought he seemed nice?"

"Jen. Stop worrying. If we get along, great. If not, no big loss, right?"

"Okay. I just really care about you, and Michael's a doll. I want it to be okay."

"It will be."

"There's just one thing. Michael's sweet and kind and hilarious. . . ."

"You told me that already. What's the *but*?"

"There's no *but*. He has a nervous tic, that's all."

"What?"

"He becomes really talkative when he's anxious. You can't shut him up. It's kind of like he's high, but he's not. I don't think he even does drugs."

"Should be an interesting night."

"Oh. No. I didn't want to freak you out. He really is a fantastic guy. He's handsome and thoughtful. He loves his parents, who are still together, I might add. And he has a great job."

"Jen. Why aren't you dating him?"

"Give me a break. Michael's an old, dear friend. It would be like dating a brother or something."

"Just asking."

"When are you two meeting up?"

"Next Friday."

"Okay. Call me and tell me how it goes."

"Will do. And stop worrying."

"Right. Take care."

"Bye."

* * *

". . . and so I told him that there was no way I was paying for the ding on his car. What a dingbat. Oh. I never thought of that. I should try to work that into a comedy routine. . . ."

Nina's tried interrupting a few times, but Michael can't seem to stop his mouth from moving. Maybe once he's more comfortable with her, he'll calm down. So Nina waits it out. In the meantime, she takes a swig of her Budweiser and studies him.

He's pretty sweet to look at: broad shoulders, slim waist, long fingers, and luscious lips. He's wearing distressed jeans that hug his ass and a T-shirt that slithers over his pecs in a way that's almost mesmerizing.

Jen was right. He's lovely. And he's sort of funny, but he's got to learn to shut up.

". . . and it was strange to find myself naked with her, you know? It was comfortable but then sort of crazy at the same. . . ."

Hold on.

"Michael," Nina says. He keeps talking.

". . . so that's why I'm so bagged today. We were up all night. We couldn't get enough of each other. It's been a while for me, so I was primed, but to be with a friend and having sex, it's like the best of both worlds. . . ."

"Michael."

". . . said she doesn't like oral sex and that's sort of strange. I mean, how could I know so much about her but not know that? And I was too uncomfortable to ask whether it's me going down on her that she wouldn't like or the other way around, so

I still don't know. I couldn't handle dating a woman who didn't enjoy that. Not that we're going to have sex again, *heh heh.* Why would I be out on this date with you?"

He stops.

Nina has a pretty good idea who he's talking about, but she needs to make sure. "Michael," she says, "are you saying you slept with Jen last night?"

He nods. Nina waits. For the first time in forty-five minutes, he's silent.

* * *

"Jen? It's Nina."

"Hey."

"So, I met Michael tonight. You were right. He's pretty chatty."

"Yeah."

"He told me about a lot of things. Like work and the car that he says he didn't ding but it's clear, even to me, that he did."

"Shit. I told him not to mention that. It's a long, boring story."

"Yes. He also told me about the wild sex you had with him last night."

"What?"

"Yup."

"Oh my God."

Silence.

"I don't know what came over us. Honest. I'm not interested in him. I mean, I never looked at him that way before. He was so nervous about this date and I was trying to calm him down and—"

"Jen. Jen. Stop. It's okay. I'm fine. I wish you had told me so I didn't waste a Friday night with him, but I'm fine. And you know what?"

"What?"

"He's perfect for you."

"You think?"

"Yes. But for God's sake, get over your oral sex issues. No man can live with that."

"What?"

Silence.

"He didn't."

"He did."

Come, give us a taste of your quality.

WILLIAM SHAKESPEARE, *Hamlet*

A Matter of Taste

IT WAS A FAIRY-TALE ROMANCE, the picture of innocence, the rosy glow of puppy love, true love. We met in grade five. Mike was the popular boy—all sinew and bravado. When he carried his lunch loose in his backpack (instead of in a childish tin box or trailer park brown paper bag), everyone followed suit. He had curly brown hair that kissed the collar of his T-shirt, and his blue eyes sparkled with an idea you just knew was so bad it had to be good. I was the budding tomboy. Tiny breasts sprouted beneath my shirt and yet I resisted training bras. Tall and lean, I swaggered in the playground with the boys, learning their secrets and carrying them to an eager audience in the girls' washroom. For a project on Japan, I brought in sushi and served it to my classmates while wearing a kimono my great-grandfather had picked up on his travels.

Amy isn't intimidating like the other girls, thought Mike. *Mike can teach me how to spit,* thought I. And thus a match was made in heaven.

None of our classmates questioned our pairing. When Mike and I (a distance of three feet between us) announced at recess that we were now boyfriend and girlfriend, the class quickly divided into two groups. The boys postured and furtively plucked underwear from their sweaty thighs. The girls giggled and skimmed their eyes over each other's bodies, assessing breast size. Mike and I raced back and forth between the groups like carrier pigeons, arranging adequate (if not love-based) matches.

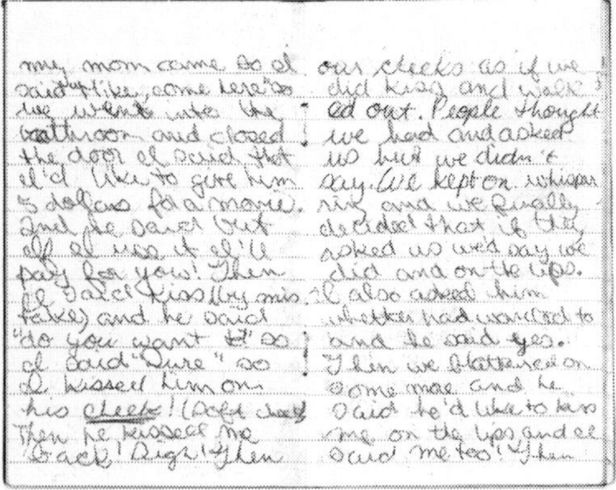

my mom came so I
said "Mike, come here" so
we went into the
bathroom and closed
the door. I said that
I'd like to give him
5 dollars for a movie.
And he said "but
if I [illegible] it I'll
pay for you!" Then
I said kiss (by mis-
take) and he said
"do you want it?" so
I said "Sure" so
I kissed him on
his cheek! ([illegible])
Then he kissed me
back! Sigh! Then

our cheeks as if we
did kiss and walk-
ed out. People thought
we had and asked
us but we didn't
say. We kept on whisper-
ing and we finally
decided that if they
asked us we'd say we
did and on the lips.
I also asked him
whether had wanted to
and he said yes.
Then we [illegible] on
some more and he
said he'd like to kiss
me on the lips and I
said "me too!" Then

Over the next two years, we gripped hands, sat stiffly in movies, hung out in the park, and held each other with sweaty palms and pounding hearts at school dances. Mike taught me to spit. I was the first girl to ever make him laugh. Though we told our mates that we had, we never kissed. And when I moved to another city, that was our biggest regret.

Years later, in university, we met again. I was running down the street to catch a bus, arms brimming with research on female circumcision, when I heard my name. Twisting in mid-stride, I saw the brown curls and the sparkling blue eyes and was twelve years old again. We hugged and I spat and he read that for what it was: a sign that I'd never forgotten, a symbol of our love. Mike suggested beer. I suggested Friday. With leaping hearts, we parted.

Friday night and we were perched on Mike's sofa. We drank beer and conversation fluttered between now and then. Van Morrison sang of heartstrings, the night's magic, and moonlight. Mike said there was something he'd been waiting years to do. My heart stopped. We kissed.

It didn't take long for us to hurl ourselves into Mike's room and lock the door. We were gripped with romantic love. We couldn't believe our luck. I, no longer as tough, had tears in my eyes. We kissed and kissed and, as Mike moved his lips down the nape of my neck, I delighted in exploring one perfect brown curl dipping into his ear. I licked at it, nibbling and tasting.

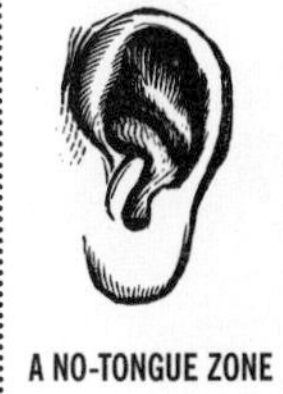

A NO-TONGUE ZONE

"What the fuck are you doing?" screeched Mike. "Are you licking my ear? That's fucking disgusting."

And that's how my fairy tale came to an end.

⁂

EVER HEAR SOMEONE TALK ABOUT a "hint of oak" or the "herbaceous flavour" of a wine and wonder what the hell they're on about? You thought it was either good or bad. Tasting wine, however, is an art. I'm sure that, given enough time, and with enough patience, I too could talk at length about the legs of a 1997 Barolo Vigna Broglio. (The real question is whether I would want to.) I just need to develop the taste.

We all have preferences. Things that, given our druthers, we'd prefer to see, eat, touch, or hear. It's what, among a few other things, makes us individuals. Over time, we figure out what we like and what we don't. Ron loves porn. Josie is set atwitter by the period romance novels of Diana Gabaldon. *Chaqu'un son gout. . . .*

As we're introduced to new things, our tastes are bound to change. It's simple when it comes to food—do you like bacon? Pork chops? Or is it more of a black forest ham kind of day? Clothes are also easy—it boils down to whether or not we look fat in them. As we lose weight after joining that women-only gym, a baby tee might actually be in the cards. (Probably not, but you see what I'm getting at here, right?) In romance, however, it takes a little longer to figure out where our predilections lie. Certain things are fixed. I'm straight. He's gay. We're bi. Other tastes lie in a murky world where boundaries are established through trial and error.

A deep, all-consuming fondness for something *can* cause problems. Men, for example, like breasts. Women know this. But if a man with a serious boob fetish tries to date a small-breasted woman with a great ass, well, she might find him narrow minded.

There are a million studies on why we like one thing over another. It's what we grew up with, what we're used to, what we experienced in past lives, blah blah blah. Who really cares why? All we need to know is that clashing tastes can kill romance faster than a fart. Add sex to the equation and nothing's gettin' nasty but the mood.

❋

DARIA IS TALL, DARK, AND HANDSOME. She's got curly black hair that's the envy of all her girlfriends. She's confident and full of fun. She's the type of woman you want as your best friend because she's fierce and loyal.

The men who fall for Daria are generally meek and unsure of themselves. The kind who nod like maniacs as she speaks and end every sentence they utter with a question mark. They like her for her strong personality, she says, because they don't have much of one themselves.

When Boris asks her out, she doesn't feel that familiar twinge in the pit of her stomach. True, she doesn't have much to go on—he just walked up to her in a bar and said, "I can't keep my eyes off you. Please agree to have dinner with me this week."

She likes his direct approach. And he's taller than her. At five-ten, Daria finds that a pleasant change. He looks, well, not nervous. Could it be that he's sure of himself?

Boris waits, unflinching, for an answer.

"I'd love to," she says. With that, Boris rewards Daria with an enormous smile.

They meet for dinner five days later. It's perfect. A beautiful, warm fall evening. A dark, romantic Italian restaurant. Plenty of red wine. No awkward pauses in the conversation. Boris is complimentary without fawning too much. Daria is fascinated by his take on things such as education (teachers should be trained in the fine arts—that way they work with different learning disabilities and help children individually) and snowmobiling (an excellent pastime as long as a woman is driving—that way no one breaks a neck).

Boris suggests that they walk back to her place and enjoy one of the last few balmy nights of the year. As they walk, he casually, without apology, puts an arm around her shoulders and pulls her close.

"I feel very comfortable with you," he says.

"And I with you," says Daria.

"Can I ask you a personal question?"

"Sure."

"What size dress do you wear?"

Hunh?

Without waiting for an answer, Boris tugs at the neck of her dress and looks at the tag. Daria has no time to react before he grins and says, "I knew it. Same size as me."

"Excuse me?"

"Do you think I might borrow this dress sometime? I think I'd look great in it," says Boris, oblivious to her distress. "Of course, I'll only wear it for you. . . ."

He winks at her. Stops. "What's wrong?"

"Uh, I'm not sure how I feel about sharing clothes with my date," says Daria. "This hasn't really ever come up before."

A look of annoyance flashes across Boris's face. "Do you have a problem with the fact that I'm a cross-dresser?"

Pink or hot Pink... what to do, what to do !?!

"I don't know," answers Daria.

"It's a free world. It's how I express myself. I feel beautiful and I look beautiful. It doesn't embarrass me, and it shouldn't embarrass you."

Daria doesn't like to be told how to feel about something.

"Boris," she begins, screwing up courage, pressing down disappointment at where this is heading. "You can do whatever you like. Wear dresses and nylons. Braid your hair. I don't care. Everyone should be able to explore different parts of their personality. I'll support you. I'll defend you." She stops to breathe.

"But just because I'll fight for your rights, doesn't mean I have to lend you my skirt."

❋

FROM: Katie
DATE: Friday, April 23, 2004 12:22PM
TO: Amy
SUBJECT: Baby's got the blues

It was the mid-1970s and I was working in Montreal. I was in journalism back then. At my office, there was a tall, blond guy that turned my eye. He was much prettier than me and wore well-cut, conservative suits. However, beneath this buttoned-up exterior, I detected a certain appealing flair.

He invited me one day to his book-lined, Victorian flat. It was impeccably decorated. Wonderful art. Expensive furniture.

Beautiful kitchen. After a quick tour, we listened to Beethoven and sipped wine while reading through newspaper listings to decide on a movie. He disappeared to change into something more comfortable.

Moments later he reappeared. He was wearing a baby-blue, one-piece velour jumpsuit. Skin tight. Nothing left to the imagination.

Ignoring my immediate urge to bolt, and against my better judgment, I accompanied him to the theatre. When our turn came to buy tickets, he skipped ahead of me and bought a single ticket—a shocker in those early days before my feminist consciousness had fully developed.

I can't remember the movie. I was too busy sinking down into my seat. I do remember the colour of the jumpsuit, though. That, I'll never forget.

*

"SO I WAS BENT OVER THIS POOL TABLE, wearing tight little cut-off jean shorts, when this guy comes up to me," says Brianna, waving a martini glass in the air. The thirty-five-year-old actress, a rising star on Canadian television, is holding court in the murky bar. At the mention of "bad date," Brianna had thrown up her arms and demanded everyone's full attention.

"I was twenty-one. That was the fashion," she says. "Imagine it: cut-off jean shorts, a pool table, a twenty-one-year-old ass. How could any guy resist?

"Anyway, he says he's a photographer and he wants to shoot me in that pose. Apparently, he was working on a series of photos of women in pool halls. I fell for it. So we start chatting. He's hot. I'm hot. It's all good.

"Back at my place, we're still just talking, nothing else has happened yet. I can't remember exactly what I was doing, only that I was getting all fired up about something. Wait . . . I think it was about those Benetton ads. Anyway, my eyes are closed while speaking.

"He says, 'Don't move. Keep your eyes closed.' I'm thinking he's going to kiss me, right? No.

"Moving out of the room, I hear him fiddling with something. That's when it hits me—I've just met this guy, brought him back to my home, and am now sitting with my eyes closed while he steals from me or gets his knife or whatever.

"So I peek. There's this guy, in my bedroom, bent over my army boots. I'm trying to figure out what he's doing when I see him pulling the laces from my boots.

"'What the fuck are you doing, man?'

"'You weren't supposed to look!'

"'We haven't even kissed yet and you were planning on tying me up?'

"He apologizes. I calm down. An hour later, we're about to have sex—again, in retrospect, not the smartest decision on my part, but hindsight blah blah 20/20, right? We're both naked, the lights are low, music is on. My hand drifts down to his penis. I've just made hand-to-cock contact when he says—and remember that this is the guy who was about to tie me up—'Oh, Brianna? That lump on my penis? It's benign. I've had it checked.'"

Brianna stops talking. Lights a cigarette, slops some martini on the table, and surveys her shocked audience.

"Yup. A lump. The size of Texas. Right on his cock.

"There was no way I could've missed it, so he had to tell me about it before I discovered it on my own. However, we're about to have sex and I'm holding this lump—what do I do? He's told me it's benign. He was upfront about it. I can't very well tell him I'm disgusted by his malformed penis." Brianna sips her drink and looks around the table. She smiles and nods her head. "Yeah, I slept with him anyway. No fireworks. I was on top. Pretty standard stuff, but the worst four weeks of waiting for STD test results."

Brianna pauses while the table erupts in laughter. "I'm clean, by the way."

*

SATURDAY, MAY 22, 12:06 A.M.

I can't believe Mike. I can't believe him! What a fucking fuck fuck fucker.

We've known each other for six years. We're good friends. Great friends. Almost best friends. We've gone camping together. We've hung out on Sunday afternoons together. We go to movies together. It's been great. But then he asks me out.

I should've known that our excellent friendship would be screwed if I said yes. What's that line in *When Harry Met Sally?* "Men and women can't be friends, because the sex part always gets in the way." So true.

So why did I say yes? Because I like him. *Like him* like him. I've had a crush on him ever since he massaged my feet that day at the restaurant. He didn't care that people were watching or that we were eating or that you don't do that sort of thing in a restaurant. He just did it because my feet hurt after walking around all day.

So for our date, we go to dinner. It's not really a *date* date because then we go to Dan's party afterwards. No one knows that we're sort of out with each other, and it's kind of fun, holding hands and pinching each other's ass when no one's looking. But then Mike goes and gets wasted. Beyond wasted. I've never seen him like that before. Granted, I've never seen him do cocaine before, either.

I'm standing by the pool, talking with Kathy, when he lurches up to me and slurs, "Gottatalktoyou. Now." He drags me off to a corner of the backyard and asks me to do a threesome with him and Steve. *Steve.* The asswipe that just broke up with my gorgeous, wonderful friend.

"No. Absolutely not," I say.

"Don't be a prude," he tells me.

I'm just seething. I'm so mad at him—I can't believe that he would ask me that before *we've* even had sex, just the two of us. And I can't believe he would think Steve, of all people, might appeal to me.

Our first and last love... Self-love.

I decide to get the hell out of Dodge. I grab my coat and I'm about to slip out the front door, without saying goodbye to anyone (especially Mike), when he appears out of nowhere and says, "Before you go, can I do a line of coke off your tits?"

Fucking fuck fuck fucker.

❋

1987.

Peta is sixteen. She looks twenty-two. Slim build, perky breasts, and long blond hair. She likes to think of herself as a rebel, and adores bad boys. On Friday and Saturday nights, she climbs out her bedroom window and shimmies down the trellis to go to bars.

Peta has had sex three times. All three were with boys her own age:

- Todd (when she was fifteen) told her he loved her. She told him she didn't think he got it in, because she couldn't feel anything.
- Sam (also when she was fifteen) was so worried about "knocking her up" he wore three condoms and then complained that he couldn't feel anything. The pimples on his back grossed her out.

- Max (when Peta was sixteen) was her boyfriend for three months, but two of those were while he was at camp. They had sex under the bleachers at school the day before he left. When he came back, he broke up with her because he'd fallen in love with a counsellor three years older than him.

Peta wants to have sex. To be precise, she wants to have good sex. She decides that the way to do this is to find an older man. In order to find an older man, she needs to go to bars.

On one of her first forays into the bar scene, she meets another Max. This Max is ancient, but she figures that, at twenty-six, he must know a thing or two about how to have sex with a woman.

It's not hard to convince him. They fumble, stumble, tumble into his bed the second time they meet. He rips her clothes off. She does the same to him. *This is it,* Peta thinks. *Now I'll know what it's all about.*

The sex is awful. It's also painful. Peta stops him after a couple of minutes. "I'm sorry," she says, "but this is really hurting me."

Max apologizes and tries to cuddle her. Peta wants nothing to do with it. She needs to get home before dawn so she excuses herself, uses the washroom, and then gets dressed. Bra, skirt, T-shirt, shoes. . . . She can't find her underwear. "Have you seen my panties?" she asks Max. Together, they hunt for them, but with no luck. Peta leaves.

Peta and Max meet three more times to have sex. All three times, the sex is crap and she stops him. Every time, Peta loses her underwear. Her last visit to Max's apartment is to accuse him of being a panty collector and to demand her underwear back. He tells her to leave.

* * *

1998.

Peta is twenty-seven. She looks twenty-two. She still has perky breasts but her blond hair is shorter. She's tired of bad boys and wants to settle down. On Sundays and Wednesdays, she jogs with Jim, a running partner she met through a local athletic store.

Jim is thirty-six. He's a lawyer and nicely built. He asks Peta to be his date at a close friend's wedding. She agrees to go with him.

On the drive to the church, Jim tells Peta that he's falling for her and would like her to consider dating him. She's never really looked at Jim in that way before—they're always both so sweaty and nasty while running that she's not inclined to think about romance.

At the reception, Jim leads Peta to their table. She's pretty much decided that she'll "give him a go"—he's considerate and looks great in a suit. His friends all seem nice, too, which is really important. He pulls out her chair and Peta sits. Jim starts to make introductions.

"We've got the best table," he says. "All of my closest friends. This is Sara and her husband, Frank. And this is Jenny with her husband, and . . ."

Peta follows Jim's gestures and stops short. ". . . my best friend, Max."

There, beaming at her from across the table, is the panty collector. He doesn't recognize her, but she remembers him. While shaking his hand, Peta squeezes it a little too hard. "Hi. I'm Peta," she says. His smile freezes. Jim interrupts to introduce her to the rest of the table.

Throughout dinner, Peta and Max avoid speaking to one another. Jim keeps encouraging conversation between them, but gives up by dessert.

At the end of the dinner and speeches, people start to excuse themselves. Jim goes off in search of another drink. Max's wife leaves to chat with a friend. Peta and Max are left alone at the table.

"So," says Peta, "you keeping up with your little hobby?"

"No," answers Max. "And these guys don't know about it."

"Not even your wife?" she asks.

"No." There's steel in his voice.

"Well," says Peta, hopping up from the table, "I hope you won't be offended if I keep my panties on tonight."

* * *

2004.

Peta is thirty-two. She looks twenty-two. As a result, everyone at the Bad Date party wants to throttle her. She's just finished telling a roomful of women about the panty collector.

"Did you ever tell Jim? Did you date Jim?"

"Did you ever see Max again?"

"What did Max's wife look like?"

Peta never told Jim, nor did she see him again after the wedding. "I couldn't be serious about someone when I know that kind of a secret about his best friend. Too weird."

Peta never saw Max again.

At the last question, Peta laughs.

"Funny you should ask. She was cute. Pretty. And when she got up from the table—granted, I may have been looking for it—she had a crazy-bad panty line."

*

"CAN MY FAMILY SUE the organizers of this conference when I die of boredom?" Diana scribbles on her notepad. A young lawyer working in a stodgy government town, Diana tried to avoid attending the highway planning conference. Unfortunately, her firm (which is hosting the event) insisted that she show up. "Your face is the face of this city," explained her boss to the groaning associates. "Be warm and welcoming. Go out of your way." *Gag.*

It's eating into my weekend, fumes Diana, as she escapes the three-hour meeting. Dodging lawyers from across the country who've descended on a local hotel, Diana works her way across the lobby. There's yet another meet-and-greet in the bar. *Meet and greet my ass,* thinks Diana. In her opinion, the week was wasted listening to lawyers spinning tales, puffing chests, and drinking too much.

Later in the day, Diana relaxes on the patio of the hotel bar. "How you doing?" A man wearing a navy blue suit and half a bottle of cologne drifts to her side. She's met Gabe, a small-c conservative, before at a previous lawyers' convention. She remembers him as nice if slightly dull.

"Tired. Bored. Fine," replies Diana.

Gabe casts about for a topic of conversation as Diana looks him over. *He's not much looks-wise,* she thinks, *but he's okay. Not really my type, but it's been a while.* She notes his Gucci shoes with approval. *I could do him,* she concludes. Sex with Gabe would definitely be better than another talk about mechanics' liens.

Gabe invites Diana to dinner. They eat. They talk. They end up back at his hotel room.

One of the first things Diana notices about him is that he's a gentleman. He's polite. Offers Diana a drink and gives her the only comfortable chair in the room. It's these small gestures that draw Diana from her seat and onto his lap.

Within half an hour, Gabe is down to his silk boxers—navy blue, of course. Diana is still in her skirt and bra when Gabe says, "It's my birthday tomorrow."

"That's nice. How old—"

Gabe interrupts. "Could you please spank me?"

Spank? No. She's misunderstood. "What?"

"Would you mind spanking me?"

Swallowing her first thought (*No way, freako!*), Diana tries to think of a kind way to let him down. What was it her boss said? "Be welcoming. Go out of your way." *Okay. Hell, why not? Maybe I'm into spanking and don't even know it.*

At the very least, she decides, it'll be a great story to tell her roommate.

Diana nods her assent and Gabe motions to the footstool. She sits and the small-c conservative lawyer lies across her lap. "Am I too heavy?" he asks.

"No. But, um. . . . How hard?"

"As hard as you like." Gabe smiles.

After a couple of smacks, Diana is silently relieved to discover that she is not, in fact, a spanker. It's kind of boring, actually. She's daydreaming about painting her bedroom in that new Martha Stewart pale green when she catches a glimpse of herself in the mirror. Her hand rising, the silk boxered bum, and the look of sheer joy on Gabe's face. She bites her tongue trying not to laugh.

She spanks Gabe for ten minutes. When her hand starts to hurt, she decides it's time to call it quits. No point in breaking a nail for this fellow.

❋

WHEN JACK ASKED ANITA if she had any pregnant friends, she didn't think too much about it. Breeding was in the air. In the past twelve months, five friends had either had a baby or become pregnant. Another two were trying. Only one girlfriend that she knew of had actually rejected babydom and gone on the pill without telling her husband.

"Yeah," Anita answered. "A couple dozen or so."

It was only later that Anita wondered why Jack had asked. *Is he that serious about me already? Holy crap. I'm not sure I'm that into him. Could I have babies with a man who smashes faces for a living?*

Jack was a boxer. A fairly good one, apparently. Anita, a film editor who knits hoodies in her spare time, knew nothing about boxing.

They met at a wrap party for a project she'd worked on. Jack was a friend of the director, and when he saw the lanky redhead in black fishnets sipping a martini, he swaggered over to introduce himself. Anita, three sheets to the wind, was overpowered by this manly, hunka hunka burnin' love. They fell into bed four hours later.

Over the past few weeks, they'd spent more time naked than clothed but were starting to get to know one another better. Jack, for example, had an endearing habit of polishing his shoes once a week. Anita, anal at heart, loved watching him hunched over his shoes, biting his tongue in concentration. When Jack found out about Anita's knitting, he teased her and then begged her to make him some leg warmers.

They were falling into a compatible relationship, and Anita definitely liked him. She was not, however, prepared to start talking babies with him. Anita wondered how to bring up the pregnancy thing with Jack the next time she saw him.

"Um, you know when you asked about pregnant friends?" she practised in her mirror. No. Too wimpy.

"Jack. I'm concerned that you're becoming too serious too soon." No. It's not like he proposed or anything.

"Hey, pregnant friends. What gives?" Perfect. She'd ask him when he was polishing his shoes.

As it turned out, Anita never needed to ask Jack. The next time they saw each other, he brought it up again. They'd just had sex and were slick with sweat. Lying on Jack's floor with the windows wide open, they fanned themselves with an empty pizza box.

"So, you know your pregnant friends?" asked Jack.

"Yeah," said Anita.

"Are any of them lactating?"

"Excuse me?"

"I mean, do you have any friends who are breast-feeding?"

"Well, yeah. Why?"

"I'm wondering if you could, you know, hook me up."

"With my friends who've just given birth?" exclaimed Anita. "Are you out of your mind?"

"No, no," laughed Jack. "With the milk. Their breast milk."

"What?"

"I like breast milk. It's really good for you and it tastes amazing. The only problem is that it's pretty hard to, you know, get your hands on."

"No shit."

"So I was wondering if you'd ask them to pump some of their milk for me."

The only answer Jack got was a slammed door.

YUM!

Masturbation, Female.

Alas, that such a term is possible! O, that it were as infrequent as it is monstrous, and that no stern necessity compelled us to make the startling disclosures which this chapter must contain! We beseech, in advance, that every young creature into whose hands this book may chance to fall, if she be yet pure and innocent, will at least pass over this chapter, that she may still believe in the general chastity of her sex; that she may not know the depths of degradation into which it is possible to fall.

WILLIAM WALLING, *Sexology*, 1904

eight

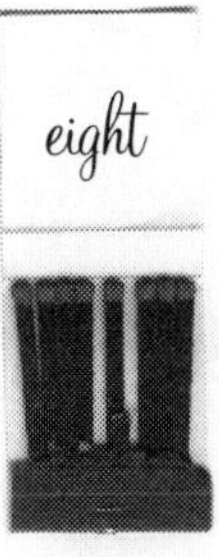

Let's Get Physical

SEVERAL YEARS AGO, I was living in Paris, France, working as a waitress at a chain of American diners called the Hollywood Canteen. I hated my job. And I'm a lousy waitress. I have terrible short-term memory and am rather clumsy, especially with piping-hot drinks. Despite these hurdles, a guy I'd met set up this job for me because I was broke. A manager at another Canteen, Jacques had a crush on me and wanted to keep me around.

A former bodybuilder, Jacques was kind yet crazy. He liked to dance around with nothing but a towel covering his "bits" (this was before we even started dating). Blond and big and prone to proposing marriage, Jacques was not my type. He pestered me for months before I agreed to go out for a drink. That's when I discovered that he had a car, which, to be honest, was the main reason I started dating him. Jacques always got me to work on time. I eventually even gave him keys so he could let himself into my apartment and wake me for work. For a time, it was an ideal arrangement.

The manager at my Hollywood Canteen was a friend of Jacques. Unlike the exhibitionist bodybuilder, Matthieu was definitely my type—a little Brad Pitt, a whole lot of bad news. He was a musician and a player.

Late one evening, while closing up, Matthieu and I found ourselves in a tight situation behind the ice cream counter. I was weak. I went home with him. Matthieu sang me songs and played his guitar. I cooed and giggled and flipped my hair. At four in the morning, we fell into bed. It was a delicious night.

I didn't, however, consider that Jacques might try to surprise me as I slept.

"Where were you?" Jacques asked when he called the next morning. I'd returned home, exhausted, to find a frantic note and increasingly urgent phone messages.

"I, uh, I was hit by a car," I improvised.

"What?"

woo	*faire la cour*
giggle	*rire (sottement)*
nibble	*grignoter*
lick	*lecher*
wild	*sauvage*
scream	*cri perçant*
better	*meilleur*
best	*le meilleur*

"Yeah, I was hit by a car. A hit and run. I spent the night at the hospital under observation."

Jacques, bless his heart, believed me. He coddled me, plumped pillows to support my head, made me tea, and massaged my feet. I felt terrible until two nights later, when, armed with a French–English dictionary, Jacques read my diary while I was asleep.

Matthieu confessed. Jacques and I broke up. I moved on. (Jacques, I hear, is now married to another Canadian named Amy.)

*

WE ALL HAVE PHYSICAL NEEDS—whether it's dry lips begging for balm, a runny nose looking for Kleenex, or an itch we'd kill to scratch. The most common need is the desperate, essential, necessary urge to pee. Especially while waiting for a bus or on a bus. We've all been there, and it's no picnic.

Some needs, let's be honest, really border on the *want* side of things. Consider the following: I need food. I need shelter. I need Matthieu. I need that new $350 Comrags dress.

This debate—wants versus needs—is examined carefully in Economics 101 and consumer studies. Obviously, it's a very human thing to confuse the two. Homebuyer help and debt control sites on the Internet offer a bunch of questions to guide you through this tricky terrain. They're not bad to consider for dating. . . .

- I feel like I really want this (him/her). Why?
- What does this thing (person) represent to me?
- Once I buy this (date this person), how will it make me feel?
- If I don't buy this (date this person), how will it make me feel?

A HIERARCHY OF NEEDS

Botox
Cute waiter
Tan leather coat
Silk beaded slip dress
Facial, pedicure, manicure & wax

If you're debating the merits of Sam over Joe, the above list is heady stuff.

When two people come together romantically, one person's needs often jam up the other's wants. And occasionally, someone's physical wants will be such that they will make the other *need* to get the hell out of there.

❋

STEPHANIE IS TRAVELLING AROUND AUSTRALIA. She's been there already for four months, and she's fallen in love with the place.

The people are hilarious and kind, the cities are fun, and the countryside is like nothing she's ever seen before.

In Melbourne, she stays at a hostel for a month. She's doing some work under the table for a couple of different businesses—waitressing and filing, that sort of thing. But her favourite part of the day is returning to the hostel. Working behind the desk in the evenings is a yummy man named Jay. Every time she comes in, Steph lingers over the tourism brochures, watching him. He's that adorable.

When Jay finally asks her out, Steph is thrilled. She's also sick as a dog. She doesn't want to risk postponing the date until her sore throat feels better, so she agrees to go. Besides, he's taking her to a World Cup qualifying soccer match between Australia and Iran. Steph loves playing soccer. It's almost as good as watching taut, buff men play soccer.

Jay and Steph get to the stadium and find their seats. In deference to the state of her throat, she just has a ginger ale. The game starts.

It's fantastic. It's such an amazing thing to watch live. Steph doesn't notice her temperature climbing. She gets a chill. Jay sees her shivering and offers her his windbreaker. It smells wonderful—all man and cologne. *Purr.* Her throat hurts more and more.

Just before halftime, an Aussie nabs the ball on a runaway play and Steph leaps to her feet to cheer. She opens her mouth and a stream of saliva flies out. She can't swallow. *When did that happen? Oh, Lord, my throat is so sore.* She doesn't want to leave, but she can't swallow her own spit any more. *Crap.*

She figures that the only way to deal with it is to hork on the ground every couple of minutes—whenever Jay is distracted by the game.

This plan works for all of five minutes. Then Jay catches her in the act. "My throat is so sore," she explains. "I can't swallow. Are you grossed out?"

"No," he says. "But I think I should take you home."

"No, no, no," she assures him. "I really want to stay. If you don't mind me spitting, I'd like to stay until the end."

Jay, looking concerned, agrees to wait out the game. He gets her another can of pop to soothe her throat. Every so often, trying to look hip, she spits on the ground. Jay squirms, looking more and more uncomfortable. Finally, the game ends.

Steph hands Jay his coat. She's fumbling with her purse in the cramped seating of the stadium when she notices his shoe. It's covered in her spit.

Stephanie is mute with embarrassment.

Jay and Steph walk back to the hostel in silence. At the door, she thanks him for the date and apologizes for being so sick. Jay advises her to see a doctor in the morning.

She does. It turns out to be an abscess on her tonsils.

Jake switches shifts at the hostel and Stephanie doesn't see him again.

*

ISABEL HAS ALWAYS HAD A THING about men who are shorter than her. It stems from grade school, when she towered over all the boys. At school dances, she was always in demand for the slow songs, since short boys could nestle their heads between her budding breasts. Looking down at their little heads snuggling close, she felt like their mother or their creepy aunt. It was awful.

Ever since, she's made it a rule to date taller men. As she is five-nine, this limits her options. From time to time, she's tried to date men the same height or shorter, but as soon as they kiss, her stomach turns. There's no romance in bending at the waist to kiss someone. That old mother/aunt feeling comes back every time.

Simon is taller than Isabel. By one inch. This, in her opinion, is borderline territory. If she wears heels, she makes sure to kick them off before the kiss. Or twist her feet sideways to rest on her ankles when he puckers up.

Simon hangs out with Isabel's crowd of friends. He's smart, funny, and a perfect gentleman—always offering to pay for drinks or food, holding out her chair, walking curbside. She's not immediately blown away by any chemistry between them or anything, but she feels quite fond of him. It's only when, while out dancing one night, Simon grabs her waist, dips her, and kisses her deeply on the lips that Isabel considers dating him. *Maybe he does have enough bite,* she thinks.

He calls the next day. *If he apologizes for the kiss, I won't date him.* He doesn't. He asks her out, and she finds herself agreeing to go for supper that night.

During the next two weeks, Isabel sees Simon five times. They have dinner, go to a movie, go for a walk in the park, go cycling. They make out in alleys, in the theatre, on park benches, and in the woods. He's become incredibly sexy. Manly and strong. Aggressive and kind. A deadly combination.

On the fifth date, he invites Isabel back to his place. She's looking forward to it—*maybe they'll actually get jiggy with it.* Walking into his apartment, Isabel is surprised. It's ordered and clean. Nothing like the chaotic mess that fills her place. His shoes are lined up at the door. Magazines are in a tidy pile on the coffee table. Garbage is empty. Simon must have cleaned up before inviting her over. She's impressed.

Isabel kicks off her shoes at the door and settles into the couch. Simon disappears into the kitchen. They sip beer for a bit and then fall all over each other. An hour later, they come up for air. Isabel's stomach grumbles so loudly that Simon climbs off of her and announces that he's going to order pizza. *Thank God. I'm starving.*

When the pizza arrives, Simon answers the door and Isabel finally rises to get plates. As she's walking past him in the hall, something feels off. He looks different. *Darker, older, or—could it be?—shorter.* On the way back from the kitchen, she stands right beside him to determine whether or not she's losing her mind. *Yup. He's shorter. At least an inch shorter. Maybe two.*

"You've shrunk," she blurts.

"Hunh?"

"You're shorter than me," she says.

Simon smiles at her. "Yes, I am," he says.

"But you weren't before."

"No. My left leg is shorter than my right by about two inches," explains Simon. "So when I'm barefoot, I'm five-eight and when I'm wearing the lift in my shoe, I'm five-ten. Is that a problem?"

This is *a dilemma. I mean, technically he's shorter, but when we're standing together, generally he'll be wearing shoes, right? But standing naked in our future home together, well, do I want to duck to kiss my husband? This is ridiculous. Simon's a wonderful guy. So what if one leg is shorter than the other? He's great. And maybe, somehow, I can just encourage him to stand on the tall leg.*

"No, no," she says. "Not a problem. Just a surprise."

They eat pizza and Isabel tries to put it out of her mind. *I can date this man. He's just fine. We're just fine.*

The phone rings. It's one of Simon's buddies, trying to lure them out with promises of beer and nachos. The sexy mood is gone, especially after devouring an enormous greasy pizza, so they agree. Simon cleans up. Isabel uses the washroom. He changes into different pants. They're standing in the front hall. Isabel crams her shoes on. Simon puts his shoes on. And then removes them.

"What's wrong?"

"I need a lift for these shoes. Shit. Where is it?"

"In there?" Isabel points to the pair of sneakers she thought he was wearing earlier.

Simon checks the insides of the shoes. "Nope. That's navy blue. I need the brown one for these shoes."

They start looking inside each pair of shoes. Isabel has a vision of herself in ten years. She's wearing a housecoat and trying to still a young child while searching for Simon's lift. *"Where's my lift, woman?"*

"Where's my lift, woman?"

Isabel waits three days and then ends it with Simon, citing confusion over a past boyfriend who's just "re-entered her life."

*

OCTOBER 13, 11:10 P.M.

I am dying. *Dying.*

I cannot stop farting. What is wrong with me?

My first date with Roger—a guy so fastidious that he keeps a Kleenex box on both the front *and* the back seat of his car—and I get gassy.

Tonight, Roger picks me up and takes me to a pasta bar for dinner. A pasta bar, of all places. If there's one dating rule that Mom drummed into me from birth, it's not to eat pasta until you are really comfortable with a man. If you have penne or those little bow-shaped ones, it's "ungainly" and "unladylike" to fit more than one on your fork at a time. Dinner, therefore, lasts three hours. If you have linguine, spaghetti, or any of the long, thin pasta, the sauce invariably flicks up without you noticing and you'll dot yourself—eyebrows, shirt, hair—with bits of it.

So, faced with unacceptable pasta, I order the first predictable thing I see on the menu. Meat loaf. Totally *unpredictable,* gassy meat loaf.

Roger's talking about his mom's cancer. How the family dealt with that blow. I fart. It's as though a runaway train of air was unleashed in my bowels—I didn't have any warning. I didn't know it was coming. I hope to God he didn't hear it, but he pauses for a second and then continues. "She's in remission now, and so we're keeping our fingers—" *Pfffft!* Another fart. Where did that come from? And how did this happen so quickly? Oh, God, I can feel another whopper building. Clench. Clench.

To this point, I have managed not to blush, but I can't focus on what Roger's saying and he's talking about serious stuff. I can't hold it in. It hurts. I've got to. . . .

"Roger. Excuse me," I say, grabbing my purse. "I've got to use the ladies' room."

He starts to ask whether he should order another round of drinks, but I can't wait to answer him. I've got to release this fart monster inside of me, so I race to the bathroom.

In the stall, I unclench. For about five minutes straight, I'm a wind machine. I've never experienced anything like this. I'd rather have a meatball stuck in my cleavage than deal with meat loaf gas. What am I going to do? This clearly isn't going to end any time soon, and so I spend ten minutes tooting and scrambling to think of a way out of this date.

"Roger," I say, feigning panic upon returning to the table. "I've just remembered that I'm supposed to prepare a statement for X Corporation to send off in the morning. I can't believe I forgot! The call came in as I was leaving work today, and I was so preoccupied that it completely slipped my mind.

I'm so sorry. I have to go home immediately and start working on it."

He makes all the right noises—*of course, I understand, we'll go right away, don't worry*. In the car, I'm so worried that he'll think I'm not interested that, even though my stomach feels like it's about to explode, I lean across the front seat and give him a kiss. An on-the-lips kiss. *Augh!* Our first kiss and all I can think about is farting.

Just writing this down is making me sick. How can one body build up so much gas? I'm still at it. An utter gastastrophe.

*

FROM: Cicely
DATE: Thursday, August 12, 2004 12:29AM
TO: Amy
SUBJECT: Thought you'd be interested in my latest blog entry . . .

I've always been amazed at my ability to have sex with perfect strangers while simultaneously being terrified of launching into something meaningful with a person I enjoy. The mere thought of the army of love conquering the territory of sex nauseates me. It's that irritating affectionate smirk that takes over a lover's face when you're looking down at them, the desperate post-coital embrace, the lame terms of endearment.

Friday night's mission to poison my precious entrails with as much liquor as possible turned two-pronged at around 11:30 p.m. That's when I realized my hair was looking good and that I could probably break a two-month dry spell and pick up some fresh-faced thing to take home. The item of choice ended up being an actor/waiter who worked at a nearby restaurant.

At 1:45 a.m., my fumbling fingers pointed at the bartender to get the table six final shots of Jägermeister. The bar closed and we stumbled home drunk. I chose the music—this is always extremely important during a one-off, as it cancels out any annoying man-noises the prey might make, and if the lay is bad at least I can focus on the syncopated rhythms of Yo La Tengo's drummer.

The actor/waiter was Evan. As is the case with most actor/waiters, he alternated between heavy narcissism and relentless self-deprecation. This is an annoying trait when you're getting down with your bad, naked bodies in the bedroom.

I pulled out a tiny Japanese silicon vibrator. It's pink and shaped like a bear. Tiny. Pink. Bear. I need to use it during sex for the usual reasons girls need to use vibrators during sex. I've never had anyone be startled or offended by it, because it is a tiny pink bear with little arms that move back and forth.

[actual size]

Evan: What's *that*?

Me: Uh, a vibrator.

Evan: What the hell are you using it for?

Me: To get off.

Evan: Well, how the fuck do you think that makes me feel?

Me: Are you serious?

Evan: Of course I'm serious.

Me: Well, I don't know. . . . This is battery operated, and you're not. I like using it.

Evan: I want you to put it away. I can't believe you pulled that shit. That's so weird.

Me: Uh, okay. . . .

So I chucked it under the bed. Evan went back to the things he had been doing. My mind started to reel. *Hold on. This guy is in* my *house, in* my *bed, getting off on* my *body, and he's telling me that I can't use a vibrator to get myself off?* I felt

I should tell him to get dressed and get out, but the Jägermeister was making my head swim. I fell asleep.

I woke up five hours later to find Evan still there. He'd gotten up and made himself a cup of tea. I waited for what seemed like an eternity for him to leave. Before he departed, Evan asked for my number. I declined.

Maybe I'm tired. Maybe it's time to settle down. I'm better off with the bear, anyway.

*

AUGUST 16.

Dear Jeanie,

How are you? I'm fine. I'm visiting my relatives in Thunder Bay, which is okay. It was pretty boring, but then I met The Most Beautiful Boy I've Ever Seen in My Life. He's so hot! He's the same age as us (he turns eighteen in September, so he's really seven months older) and he has sandy hair and dark colouring, kind of like Tom's but better, you know? Totally my dream boy. I think I'm in love. His name is Rory and he knows my uncle. I think he does some work for him sometimes. Or something like that. Anyway, he's so gorgeous that I think I sounded like a twit. I just said, "Hey," and that's it. He probably doesn't even remember me.

Gotta go. My aunt is calling me for dinner. Will write later.

Bye,

Mary

* * *

August 18.

JEANIE!!!!!!!

OMG, OMG, OH MY GOD!!! RORY ASKED ME OUT!!!

He just called and I am soooooo excited. I'm totally in love with this guy. And he's gorgeous! He wants to take me "driving." That totally means he wants to fool around, right? I could even lose my virginity to him, he's that hot.

We're going out tomorrow night. YAY!!

Have to go. I've got to figure out what I'm going to wear. Maybe the flared jean skirt that makes my ass look bigger.

Will write you *all* the details,

Mary

* * *

August 19.

Dear Jeanie,

Life sucks.

How are you? I'm a loser. I wish you were here.

I went on the date with Rory the Cute. He picked me up and was as gorgeous as I remembered. He was all cool and polite with my aunt and uncle and then we went driving.

About ten minutes after we got in the car, I realize that I have to pee. Really, really badly. But we're driving. And driving. It gets to the point where pee is going to start bursting through my belly button, but there's no way I can admit to needing to whiz.

I need to pee so badly that I think I'm going to throw up, so I suddenly say, "Stop, I'm going to be sick." He pulls over in some parking lot and I go around the back of the building. He was so sweet, asking me if I needed help. Oh my God. I can't even think about it. Why am I such an idiot? Obviously, I told him no.

I race around to the back of the building, find some bushes, and pee. It takes forever. I keep thinking he's going to come and find me with my pants around my ankles, so

I'm trying to pee harder but just end up hitting my shoes. So gross.

Anyway, when I get back to the car, I'm so embarrassed. As I'm wiping my mouth, pretending that I just threw up, I realize that Rory would totally rather kiss someone who'd peed over someone who'd just puked. He drives back to my uncle's house.

I'll repeat: I am a fucking idiot.

Mary

❄

"DEE?"

"Hey, Ruth."

"So, did you lose it?"

"Lose what?"

"Oh, c'mon! Your cherry. When I left you last night, that was the plan, remember? You. Dave. Booze. 'I'm tired of being the only virgin I know.' Anything coming back to you?"

"Yeah. I know. Quick, meaningless sex so I could get it over with, but he was a jerk."

"Dee. He's in the army. What did you expect?"

"Remember when I was talking to him at the bar and you interrupted us to get me to dance? Well, he was telling me this story about how a girl wouldn't have sex with him, so he jiggled the bed all night so she couldn't sleep."

"And you still went home with him?"

"I thought it was funny at the time, but I think that was the beer. Besides, I had picked last night to be The Night and he was hot."

"True. He was hot."

"So, we had another drink and then went back to his place. I figure I'm drunk enough now to just go for it. We whip off our clothes and start making out. He's trying to get it in and it hurt. I called it off."

"What did you say?"

"Lied. Told him he was too big. I figured he'd be pretty chuffed. Anyway, I start to fall asleep and the jerk starts jiggling the bed. I told him to cut it out. He said he 'needed it' and that I was blue-balling him. So I moved to the floor."

"You didn't."

"Yup. I grabbed a blanket and pillow and curled up on the floor. But he kept jiggling the bed so it would creak, you know? What a jackass. And I couldn't get out of there because I didn't have enough money for a cab. Besides, I was way too loaded. And tired."

"So what did you do?"

"Slept in the bathtub."

*

"I WAS AT THIS CATHOLIC WEDDING," Roberta starts, "and this completely ordinary, half-bald, tubby guy caught my eye."

Roberta is tall, blond, and gorgeous. An employee at a successful public relations firm, Roberta has everything a man could want—looks, brains, money, and independence. For some unfathomable reason, she goes on the worst dates. She's rotten at picking men.

You are open-minded and quick to make new friends.
Lucky Numbers 11, 16, 27, 33, 36, 44

Sitting around a table are a group of her close friends. If there's one thing these women know about their evenings together, it's that Roberta will have a bad-date story to tell. At this particular dinner are two women who haven't heard all of her stories, and so Roberta was encouraged to tell her "Eenie Weenie Peenie" story. A Roberta classic.

"I don't know why this guy caught my eye," she says, spearing a spring roll with a chopstick. "No, I know why. He was the only one who got up to take Communion. That's it. He was very religious. So I chatted him up at the reception and he gave me his number. I've been bad and gone out with men I shouldn't have, so I thought I should go out with a nice guy, a church-going, conservative man.

"Our first date was dinner. It was nice. Our second date was Shakespeare in the Park. A couple more dates and I was starting to feel obligated to be his girlfriend.

"He invited me up to his cottage for a weekend and I was unsure. I liked him. He was nice, but boring. I said yes and then I was mad at myself for accepting. Anyway, I was a bitch the entire way up to his cottage and, as a result, once we got there, I had guilt sex.

"It didn't take long. Before I even knew what had happened, it was over. Thirty seconds, tops. He was so overwhelmed.

"I'm lying there, stunned that he's all done, and I feel this wetness that I shouldn't be feeling. I look down and realize that the condom is still inside me. His penis fell right out of it. His cock was the size of his little finger. It was tiny. It was—"

All of the women interrupt her and chorus, "The eenie weenie peenie!"

"Exactly. Now, I know that size isn't supposed to matter, but it does matter if you can't feel anything. And there was nothing, absolutely nothing, in it for me. And that decided it for me. No peenie? I'm a meanie.

"I tell him that it just isn't working for me and he says, 'Yeah. I didn't think so. Making love to you was my last-ditch effort.'

"Sad. Very sad. I almost agreed to another thirty-second round of guilt sex."

The signs of the enjoyment and satisfaction of the woman are as follows: her body relaxes, she closes her eyes, she puts aside all bashfulness, and shows increased willingness to unite the two organs as closely together as possible. On the other hand, the signs of her want of enjoyment and of failing to be satisfied are as follows: she shakes her hands, she does not let the man get up, feels dejected, bites the man, kicks him, and continues to go on moving after the man has finished.

KAMA SUTRA

nine

Dirty Girl

MY ASS IS IN THE AIR. And it's being slapped.

How on earth did I find myself in this position? I hadn't planned on this. When I met up with Leo for supper, I wasn't thinking, *How best to have my ass slapped tonight?* I was thinking, *Should I have steak or salmon?*

I've known Leo for years. We're good friends who flirt. Obviously, we're attracted to one another. How else does this sort of thing happen? But we've never really pursued it. We're both sort of lazy that way.

Yesterday, he left a message on my machine to say he was coming to town. "Hello, beautiful girl. I'm coming to see you. Eat? Drink? Laugh? Say yes." The last time I'd heard his voice was six months ago. I called him back and we arranged a "meet 'n' eat."

I chose salmon. It was a good choice. Lots of lemon and capers and butter and loveliness. And the wine was great. A Cabernet Sauvignon—full bodied, a hint of bumbleberry pie and cocoa (I'm not kidding, the waiter actually said that). I know you're not supposed to drink red wine with salmon but, in my opinion, when you can have red, why drink white? *Ouch.* Leo's getting even more enthusiastic.

The wine is what led me here. It's the wine's fault, really. There was the bottle (okay, we had two) and it tasted good. And the food was delicious. And the conversation was fun. For the first time in what felt like months, I'd laughed really hard, tears squeezing from the corners of my eyes. And then Leo had to lean across the table, pluck a trapped tear from my lashes, and suck on his finger. Well. When someone does such a thing, it's hard to resist. Especially when they're staring at you in a way that makes you feel sexy and yet still understood.

Don't blame me.

He's staying in a terrible fleabag hotel, which makes me feel, with my ass in the air, more seedy than desirable. Especially since my mind has decided to leave and wander down this rambling road. At least if the room were nice, I could marvel at the wrinkle-free bed linens while Leo works his very own special sort of magic.

I would stop him, you know, if I thought I could do that without damaging his self-esteem. I mean, I'm nearly wetting the bed, I'm giggling so hard, but he's thinking that this excites me. "Oh, yeah, you like that, don't you?" When he said that— Whoops, he just said it again. And I can't stop laughing. Oh, this is terrible. Hold on while I stuff a pillow into my mouth so he can't hear me laugh.

How can he be so bad? He's very sexy. His kisses are spectacular. Do other women like this? Maybe I'm a freak. Maybe I'm a prude. Okay, I'll try to enjoy it. . . . Nope. Nothing's happening here for me. Da boy, he ass-slappy. Tee hee. I'd love a picture of this, except then I'd have to burn it.

What I would give to be home in bed with some cinnamon toast. Let's see, I'd give. . . . A car alarm. Hey, I'm not so drunk that I can't see my way out of here.

"Um, excuse me, Leo? I think that's my car. I've got to check. Sorry, sorry. I've got to go and see. Whoops, did I just kick you? Sorry about that. I'll just, no, no, don't worry. Let me check. Damn, where's my shirt? I can't have my car broken into again. I know, the timing sucks. I'm sorry but I really can't afford. . . . Where's my shoe? Have you seen my shoe? What? Oh, I had one installed a few months ago. Because of the other break-in. A few months ago. Bloody vandals. What's this world coming to? So dangerous. But it's really been so nice to see you. It stopped? Shit. I mean, it does that after a couple of minutes but they could still be looting it and I'd better. . . . What? No, no. I didn't take a taxi. I drove, don't you remember? Yes. I drove. It's in the parking lot. At the back end. Why am I giggling? I just do that when in a rush. Nervous tic. Oh, don't walk me to the car. Safest city in the world, really. Take care. Kisses. Bye."

WE WANT TO BE DIRTY. We want to be fucked. And then push comes to shove, and beyond "do me, do me now," what else is there to say? No one teaches us these sorts of things. There's no Emily Post etiquette chapter on how far a nice girl can go before she becomes irretrievably dirty. And the things we could learn from pornos, strip bars, *really* nasty girls, don't work for us. How does one wrap her mind around Kiki's trick with a rubber glove and a garden hose? C'mon, give us a break. We still need our sleep. We need to work in the morning and have supper with our parents.

We want to be dirty, but not too dirty. It's a vicious circle.

It's no wonder that, more often than not, when we try to be dirty, we fail. We cannot keep up the role of dirty girl without dissolving into fits of laughter, disgust, or embarrassment. For example, a girl may want to beg for cock but, ideologically, she doesn't want to be demeaned, and she certainly doesn't want her man to think that she needs it or really even wants it that badly because, really, she could get it anywhere and he should feel lucky that she's into him and not his friend. See how hard this is?

*

FROM: Tara
DATE: Thursday, February 12, 2004 6:20PM
TO: Amy
SUBJECT: Dirty Talk Man

I met him at a friend's party. We had a wonderful conversation. We talked all night about music, travelling, politics, and reincarnation. We argued about whether you should turn down the pages of your books or leave them pristine and use a bookmark (I vote for turning down).

As the party was winding down, he asked me to come with him to a neighbouring bar for a nightcap. He actually used the word *nightcap,* which always makes me laugh—I think of an elf wearing a stocking cap and boozing it up.

We walked to this dark little bar, the kind with candles shoved into empty wine bottles, and found seats in the corner. There were maybe four other people there, and so we had a very attentive waiter. We ordered some drinks and kept talking about books and then moved on to our favourite films.

This guy put away a number of nightcaps and then out of nowhere—*BOOM!*

"Know why I asked you here?" he said, as his boozy breath washed over me. "Because I want to fuck your cunt till you scream my name."

"Excuse me?"

"You heard me, you nasty girl. I want to come all over your tits and rub my ass down your back. I want you to beg for more . . . ," he continued for several minutes while I sat there wondering if I'd heard him correctly. Was he joking? Was he imitating some film scene that I wasn't familiar with? Was he being ironic?

This raunchy stuff burst out of him in a torrent. Even though I hadn't said a word to encourage him, he kept spewing dirty talk.

"I want you to stuff my underwear into your mouth and moan like an animal. . . ."

I'm my mother's daughter. I left money on the table for my drinks and got out of there as fast as I could.

FRIDAY, 11:46 P.M. What's going on inside Elizabeth's head:

It's going to happen. It's really going to happen this time. Okay. Breathe. I'm cool. I'm calm. I'm hot. I must be hot if I'm about to have a threesome, right? You can't be a true dyke until you've had a threesome. Unwritten rule or something. A rite of passage. An unforgettable moment marking the beginning of a whole new world. I'm about to enter a whole new universe of sex. I can't wait. Really. I've tried to make this happen before. It's a hard subject to bring up. I'm not very good at picking women up. I don't know what to say. Bess just sidled over to Kelly. "Come home with us," she said. Then she kissed her. Wow. So that's how it's done. Bess is the shit. She knows how to do stuff that I've never even thought about doing. Like funnelling water from the sunroof of her car while on a rainy road trip. "I like to have fresh water at hand," she says, as if it's normal to have a tarp, plastic cone, and water jug hooked up to the ceiling of your car.

So here we are. In the cab. Bess is between me and Kelly. That's good, because I'm sort of frightened by Kelly. She's a babe. I'm so nervous I keep jumping whenever Bess puts a hand on my leg. Relax. Be cool. How do we know what to do to whom? Don't be stupid. I've had sex before. It's not like there's a guidebook to threesomes. I'll get the hang of it, I'm sure. I'll be fine. God, it's hot in here. I'm almost sleepy. Wait a second. Hold the phone. Body, brain, listen to me. Don't you dare fucking conk out on me, got it? This is a big night. Don't fail me now. Don't do this to me tonight. Not again.

I can't stop sweating. Out of the cab, easy does it. Now, I've just got to walk. I do it every day. No different now. Oh. Kelly's kissing me. That's sort of sudden. Okay. Nice. I like this. Oh. Yeah, this is good. I'm cool. How did we get inside? Oh. Oh. This is very cool. I'm in a threesome. I'm in a girl sandwich. Shit. Warm in here. Is the heater on? Yikes. Hot. Wow. Oh. Good. Like riding a bike. Or, not really riding a bike 'cause I've never done this before, so what's the analogy for this? *Oof.* A knee in my stomach. This bed is soft. Tired. Don't. Hot. Shouldn't fall asleep. Very rude. Man, it's hot. . . .

For the third time in a year, Elizabeth falls asleep during an attempted threesome. Suffering from a nervous condition that puts her under whenever she experiences stress, Liz is now known in the lesbian community as "sleeping beauty." She hasn't worked herself up for a fourth attempt. Yet.

*

OH, THIS IS NICE. *Better than nice. This is just fabulous. Ben kisses like a rock star. He kisses like a serpent—ew, that's gross. He kisses like an expensive Swiss chocolate. Oh. So good.*

Martha is lounging on her tan leather sofa. On top of her, caressing her neck with his lips, is Ben. Lovely, hot Ben.

This is their third date and, so far, it's going very well. When Martha buzzed him up to her apartment, she raced to put the pasta water on. She was going to woo him with her cooking skills. But Ben had a different idea. He swaggered in the door, grabbed her around the waist, and announced, "I'm making love to you all night long."

How does a girl say no? Really, it's not polite.

What cologne is he wearing? It's enough to make me melt. And these shoulders—he must be a rower or something. Mental note: ask about favourite sports. If I'm dating a rower, then I've died and gone to heaven. Stop thinking!

Ben is reaching for the button on Martha's skirt when she remembers the pasta water.

"Wait!" She lets herself slip from the couch and lands with a plop on the floor. "I've got the burner on. Let me turn it off."

Catching her reflection in the mirror, she's amused by what she sees. Her curly auburn hair is standing almost on end and there's lipstick smeared across her face. She's never felt such an animal attraction to someone before.

Where did he go?

When Martha returns to the living room, having turned off the pasta water, Ben is not in sight. She glances at the bathroom door—it's open. She peeks into her bedroom and there he is, lounging on her bed, shirt off and the top button of his jeans undone.

He's like a work of art. He's a sculpture by Michelangelo. Oh, be still my heart. Be calm my loins.

Do you, like, row?

Ben looks up and offers Martha a lazy grin. He pats the bed beside him and she floats across the room. Within twenty seconds, they're devouring each other. *Whoosh!* Off with her shirt. *Bam!* His watch hits the floor. *Zip!* Lose those jeans. *Swish!* Her skirt puddles around her feet. They're down to their skivvies and Martha wants to rip off his boxers.

Leaning across her, his slightly hairy but not hirsute chest pressing in a delightful way against her breasts, Ben twists the knob on the light, immersing them in near darkness.

"Hold on," says Martha, again slipping out from underneath him. "I'm going to light some candles."

There's no way I'm not *going to see his ass. I've waited a week to see this butt. And that lovely soft spot between his angular hip and his, uh, family jewels? I'm kissing that spot for sure.*

She lights some vanilla-scented candles that she bought at the dollar store and then pounces on Ben. She unhooks her bra and flings it across the room. He's mesmerized. *Good.* She hooks her thumbs into his underwear and pulls it down. *This man is in for a treat. I'm going to give him the best blow job ever.*

She kisses him and then, like a cat, works her way down his body, purring and licking and kissing. She gets to his penis. *Aha! Well done, my boy. Well turned out. Wait. What is that? Holy fuck. He's bleeding. He's bleeding!*

"Um, Ben?"

"Mmmhmm?" He's preoccupied with her breasts.

"Uh, I think you're bleeding."

"What? No. I'm fine."

"No. I don't think so. There's a really nasty-looking thing on your penis. It's red and there's blood all around it. It looks pretty awful. I think you should have a look."

Ben stops playing with her nipples and gives her a hard look. Pulling himself into a seated position, he takes a deep breath.

"Nasty looking? Pretty awful?"

"Yeah." *Why doesn't he look worried? I'd be freaking out if that were my penis. He's so calm. . . .*

"That would be my birthmark."

"Oh."

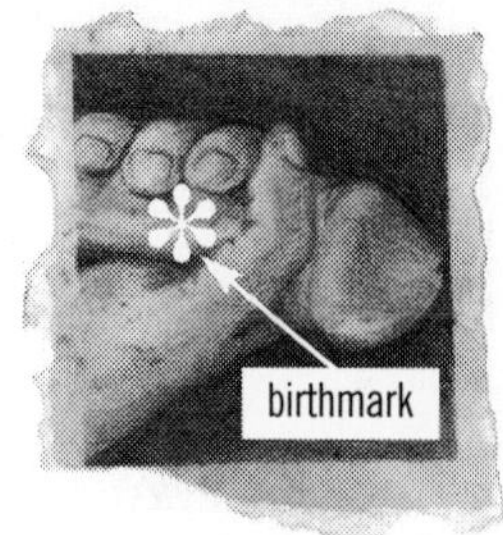

Ben slips out from beneath Martha. Grabbing his underwear from the floor, he yanks it on, a look of fury and embarrassment on his face. Martha searches for words, gestures, anything she can do to apologize. Ben rummages through the clothes on the floor and finds his jeans.

"I'm sorry. I didn't know. Don't go. It doesn't matter."

"Nasty? Awful? God forbid I should ask you to deal with that." Grabbing his watch and shirt, Ben stalks out of the room. Martha can't find any words.

The front door closes with a soft thud.

*

JULY 13, 3:33 A.M.

I ended things with Rob tonight.

I'm doing okay. I'm not upset. We're really not right for each other—that much was made crystal clear tonight—but I dread going back into the single world. I hate dating. The "what do you do"s and the "what do you like"s, because it's all so false.

This one lasted two months. Not bad. Obviously, it takes two months before you really get to know someone, so that makes returning to the dating game all that more difficult.

Honestly, though, two months isn't very long. Could be better. And if Rob hadn't asked me to do that . . . thing tonight, we'd still be together. I wonder if that makes me a prude? Am I uptight? Maybe that's why I have such trouble finding someone

I'm compatible with. I'd like to think that the guys I date are all screwed up, but maybe it's me who needs therapy.

Actually, that's why I agreed to Rob's request tonight. I thought it might be something I was into, and I also didn't want to reject him outright. I never would have known I liked asparagus if Mom hadn't made me eat it.

This is what Rob thinks is my problem. When I broke up with him, he said that I'm over-analytical. "You think too much." How that can be a fault, I have no idea. And what does it mean, anyway? We're taught—no, *trained*—to think things through before we do anything. Look both ways before you cross the street. Don't tell the lady she's fat. Don't wear skanky clothes or else people will think you're easy.

Rob told me that I need to loosen up.

It was strange tying Rob up. I didn't know how tight the silk scarves should be—too loose and he's going to think I'm not really trying, too tight and the blood flow to his extremities might be jeopardized. I also didn't want to rip my scarves. Dad brought them back from Italy. Rob kept moaning softly while I was tying him. I wasn't really touching him, but he was so turned on.

The makeup part was what really threw me. When a guy asks you to tie him up and put makeup on him, does that mean foundation? Or does he just want the basic lipstick, liner, and blush that guys think is all that women use? I tried to ask him, but he shushed me. I hate that.

Dry, oily or combination?

Deciding on a shade of lipstick was tough. Garish? Or a colour that would really suit him? He might simply have wanted to look pretty, but I don't think so—as soon as I touched the lipstick to his lips, his erection bounced. He was harder than I've ever seen him, too. That's a bit off-putting, to be honest: a guy more turned on by your makeup than you.

By the time we got to the photos, I was bored of it all. "Take another," he kept telling me. He lost the "mood," though, when, unable to take any more pictures, I told him that I hoped he was going to reimburse me for the roll of film.

❋

IF EYES ARE THE WINDOWS to the soul, then Nick's soul is pure liquid sex. Thick lashes surround deep brown pools of toe-curling ecstasy. He has movie star eyes, always moist, with the lids at half-mast. Leah is staring at him. Sitting at the bar, nursing a Stella Artois, Nick's eyes brush over Leah's body.

She shivers.

Nick is older than her by about fourteen years. He's a bar hound. He's separated, but not divorced. He's in here almost every night. Leah's never talked to him before, but she knows all of these things. She's been eyeing Old Liquid Eyes for months.

She doesn't care about his issues. The place is packed and she sees her chance. Leah sidles up to the bar, takes a deep breath, and perches on a stool. "I'm Leah," she says.

"Nick."

"I know."

He nods and motions to the bartender to bring Leah a beer.

"Where are your friends?" asks Nick.

"I'm early," shrugs Leah.

"Want to smoke a joint?"

"Sure."

Leaving their bottles on the bar, Nick and Leah walk to the door and squeeze past the lineup of people waiting to get in. They head around the side of the building. An ancient, rusty metal fire escape climbs the side of the bar. Halfway up is an exit onto the roof of a shack attached to the main structure. Leah's been here twice before. Nick nods at the group of people clambering down the stairs.

As Nick rolls a joint, Leah looks out over the parking lot. They've got the roof to themselves. They don't talk much, but Leah's mind is racing. She can't stop shivering whenever Nick looks at her.

Leah is not the type to do anything rash. She plans for road trips by cleaning out the cooler and packing it with ham sandwiches, fruit, juice boxes, and napkins. She always brings a first aid kit when camping. She's the one who tamps out the fire before crawling into her sleeping bag.

Deep down inside, however, Leah's a rebel. Sometimes she leaves the blinds up on purpose while changing because she knows her married neighbour watches her. She masturbates in the bathroom at work. Once, she told people she was going away on a business trip but actually spent the weekend with a friend's brother in a motel on the edge of town.

She's starting to feel the effects of the marijuana. Nick asks her something, but she doesn't hear it. She's drowning in his eyes. She leans over and catches one of his eyebrows in her mouth. Nick reaches for her and they melt to the roof of the shack.

Leah tugs her shirt open. Nick devours her breasts. Grabbing a fistful of hair, she yanks his head back to stare into his eyes. Nick pulls her onto his lap. They nip at each other's mouths. Nick sucks. Leah unzips. They are panting and savage.

Leah pulls up her skirt and straddles Nick. He growls. She laughs. He moans. She gasps.

It's all over in five minutes. Five fantastic minutes.

They beam at each other on their rooftop love nest. Leah tweaks Nick's nipple.

"I should find my friends," she says.

"I should get back to my beer," he laughs.

They are slow to rebutton, rezip, return.

Leah kisses Nick one final time before adjusting her skirt and descending the staircase. They walk to the door and a hushed crowd parts for them. Someone twitters. Someone else whistles.

Leah stops in her tracks. She catches sight of her friend Deb in the lineup. Biting her lower lip, Deb points behind Leah to the shack.

Leah turns.

Past Nick, across the parking lot, Leah looks up at the shack. From where she stands, surrounded by a crowd of fifty, the moon is shining down, spotlighting the roof. Leah can see it perfectly.

The crowd breaks into applause.

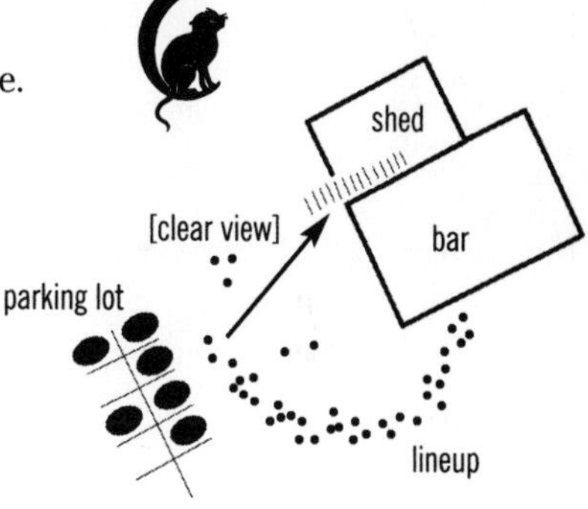

If you, your friends, or your relatives are sick, do not bore him with the details. Any mention of illness is unmysterious.

Yvonne Antelle, *How to Catch and Hold a Man,* 1966

Love Hurts

EACH STEP ON THE ROAD kicks up a swirl of dust motes. Brown grass wilts at the pavement's edge. Paint curls on the clapboard houses. The sun beats down on everything, draining moisture from the world. I'm parched. Licking my cracked lips, I scuff my way over to Nate, who is leaning against an electrical pole.

We're sixteen years old and on a week-long geography field trip to the United States. Our parents believe that we're learning about the venerable history of stalactites and stalagmites. In truth, we've figured out how to crack the pointy tips off the nationally protected formations and bounce our voices around the caverns.

In our off time, we shuttle from corner store to corner store trying to buy alcohol with fake ID made by someone's older brother. Or we fall in love.

Nate is from a broken home. His father disappeared years ago and left his mother, a wisecracking redhead, to raise two children in a tiny apartment above a Vietnamese grocer. Nate loves his mother, smokes, and runs around naked in graveyards to impress girls.

My home is peaceful. My parents are still together. I find it boring. That's why I'm walking down the road behind our motel toward Nate's hunched back. I crave excitement.

In the oppressive heat, I hear the wet smack of blood hitting the ground before I see it. Looking down, I see a tiny pool collecting at Nate's feet. As I watch, another droplet falls and, for a split second, the edges of the blood curl up, revealing dusty undersides.

"Nate? You okay?"

He stiffens and turns even further from me. "Yeah."

"Are you bleeding?"

"Yeah."

"Do you need help?"

"Yeah."

"I'll go get Mr. Donald."

"No. Don't. I don't need him."

"But. . . ."

"No, Amy. I only need . . . you."

Nate turns to face me. Crickets chirp and flies buzz. Embarrassment is etched on his face. I look down and see how love manifests itself in Nate.

AM\ is carved into his arm.

"I couldn't finish the Y because it was really starting to hurt. But I love you. I know you'd never want to date me, and I wanted to remember this pain. . . . Um, maybe we should go get Mr. Donald. I'm feeling kind of faint."

I WAS A SUCKER for the old carving-my-name-in-his-arm trick. I dated Nate for the next eight months. And whenever we snuggled on the benches in the courtyard during our lunch break, I'd run my finger along the scar and sigh.

The angst of teenage love is all consuming. We're willing to do anything—embarrass ourselves, compromise ourselves, lose ourselves. And nothing can compare to the pain of a teenage heart breaking, but we sort of expect the intense physical agony at that age. We want to feel *everything* all the time.

When we're older, physical pain (especially that requiring medical attention) is just plain frightening. When we're stressed about romance as well as work and making car payments, pain in the heart region could be gas, high blood pressure, or a heart attack. By this age, physical shortcomings make us human, and we now know that humanity is ugly.

Sometimes, no matter what you do, accidents happen. You can have the best intentions and plan every minute of a special date, but then something throws you off and suddenly you're in the emergency room. You're late, try to apply mascara while driving, stab yourself in the eye while almost missing a stop sign, and crash your car. He finds you funny, he chokes on a meatball, the waiter performs the Heimlich manoeuvre, and the regurgitated meatball lands in your hair.

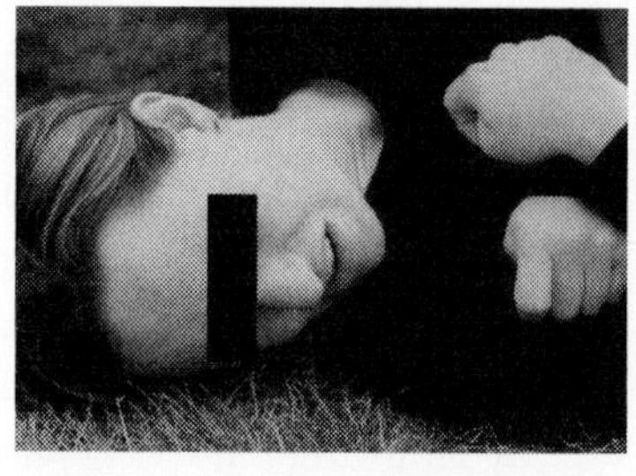

*

MARGARET IS RUNNING LATE.

It's her first date with Michael, so after work she'd gone shopping for a new pair of shoes. Somehow she ended up at her aesthetician's, dyeing her eyelashes and getting a quick manicure.

"Crap, crap, shit," she yells, stubbing her toe on the closet door. Margaret whips off her work clothes and shimmies into a new slip dress. She checks the time. Five minutes until Michael is due. Grabbing her new shoes, Margaret applies some Lip Venom as she stumbles down the stairs. Where's her purse?

Three hours and a bottle of Wolf Blass Cabernet Sauvignon later, Margaret is having a fantastic time. She could care less about mergers and acquisitions, but she *was* impressed by Michael's knowledge of wine. They both love murder mysteries and OutKast's Andre 3000. The date is going so well, in fact, that Margaret plans to invite him in for a drink when he drops her off at home.

In the car, Margaret tallies the number of "accidental" touches that have occurred during the evening: her hand while pouring the wine, knees knocking under the table (that could be explained by his long legs), her neck when Michael lifted her hair above the collar while helping her on with her coat (excellent manners), and the small of her back as they left the restaurant. Nice. Very nice.

Suddenly, they're on her stoop and Margaret squirms as she searches for a non-cheesy way to ask Michael inside. "Uh, do you want to come in?" she blurts.

He smiles, reaches for her waist, and draws her toward his lips. They kiss. She moans softly. Michael pulls back and Margaret goes weak in the knees. Literally. In one swift movement, Margaret collapses on the ground.

"Margaret?" says Michael.

An hour later, Margaret wakes up in the hospital.

* * *

When Margaret is released, she finds Michael slouched in the hospital's emergency waiting room, holding his left hand and looking bewildered.

"Hi," she says.

Michael leaps to his feet and asks her how she's doing. "I'm so sorry," he adds. "I completely fucked up."

"What happened?"

He ushers her to a seat.

"Well, I kissed you. Do you remember that?"

Margaret nods.

"You collapsed. Unconscious. I didn't know what was going on, so I tried shaking you and calling your name, but you weren't moving. Anyway, I was freaking out. No one was around and so I rummaged through your purse—sorry about that—to find keys or a cellphone or something."

As Michael is speaking, Margaret does a mental tally of the contents of her purse: lipstick, compact, wallet ($64, Visa card, and driver's licence with that awful photo—oh, no), used Kleenex (gross), matches, PDA, earrings, perfume, tampons (oh, God, no), and an EpiPen.

"That's when I found the EpiPen," Michael says. "I didn't know you were allergic."

Margaret shrugs. What is she supposed to say?

"Your Medical Alert bracelet lists your allergy as peanuts. I was pretty sure you hadn't had peanuts at dinner. And I figured you would be pretty careful about what you ordered. I didn't want to use the EpiPen if it wasn't an allergic reaction.

"Your eyes were swelling shut and your lips turning blue. I thought you were dying.

"And then I remembered: I ate a handful of peanuts earlier in my race to get out the door to meet you. I'm so sorry."

Michael had never used an EpiPen before. Calling for help, his voice cracking, he whipped off the cap and shook it. That seemed like the right thing to do. Holding out his left hand to feel whether any liquid had started to drip from the needle, Michael became aware of a sharp pain. Looking down, he saw the EpiPen sticking out of his palm.

It had discharged into his hand.

Margaret's neighbour had heard his shouts, explains Michael, and she called 911.

Despite the initial chemistry, there's no shot of adrenalin that can revive their romance. They do not see each other again.

How to use an EpiPen

1. Take cap off.
2. Stab allergic person with needle. Aim for side of thigh, halfway between knee and hip.
3. Do NOT test first.

❄

FROM: Tamara
DATE: Tuesday, July 13, 2004 2:05PM
TO: Amy
SUBJECT: Worst date ever

I was bartending in London while attending university. Sally's friend Lucas expressed interest in me and asked Sally to set us up. After a few months of saying no, I decided to give this Really Nice Guy a chance ("really nice" was not a quality I looked for in a mate—at the time, I preferred big, ugly, and selfish).

On a snowy night in November, Lucas showed up at my front door with chocolates for me and dog biscuits for our house dog. It was painful.

We went for a lovely meal at La Cabana and then toodled off to the Spotted Duck for some drinks. Things were great—relaxed, informal, fun—but there was, as I'd predicted, no spark.

Lucas excused himself to go to the washroom and I waited at the bar. Five minutes passed. Ten minutes. . . . *What was taking him so long?* Fifteen minutes. *Could it be? Had I just been abandoned in the middle of a date by such a nice guy?* After twenty minutes, I was worried.

I asked the bartender if he would mind taking a quick

peek in the men's washroom to make sure everything was okay. "Be subtle," I told him. If Lucas was constipated, I didn't want him to feel any more, ahem, pressure.

The washroom was down a flight of stairs. A few seconds after the bartender descended, he reappeared in an absolute frenzy. Panting from running up the stairs, he called 911.

Twenty minutes earlier, an old, boozy fellow had walked into the washroom as Lucas was washing his hands. While peeing, the drunk suffered a heart attack and crashed into the urinal, busting his head open on the porcelain. Lucas screamed for help as he performed CPR. It was, however, a quiet night, and there were no visitors to the loo. We couldn't hear him over the music upstairs.

He who expects no gratitude shall never be disappointed.
Lucky Numbers 4, 8, 23, 32, 34, 39

Lucas revived the old fellow within a minute or two and was promptly rewarded with projectile vomit. He yelled for help for thirteen minutes. The paramedics arrived, transferred the old drunk to hospital, and thanked Lucas. He'd saved this man's life.

Covered in blood and vomit, Lucas insisted on walking me home.

I see him once in a while and we laugh about our terrible date. How is it that such a nice guy, a hero, didn't arouse any interest on my part? I am truly a terrible, terrible human being.

*

"HEY, MOM. IT'S ME."

"Ella, darling. How are you?"

"I'm okay."

"No, you're not. What's wrong?"

"Nothing. Just another bad date."

"Oh, dear. Who was it with?"

"This guy. Tom. He's a friend of Cathy's. Mom, I'm so tired of this. I'm tired of being a thirty-two-year-old single woman. It's awful. I might as well get five cats and call it quits."

"It can't be that bad."

"All the hot, interesting guys want firm, taut, young bodies. Women who cover their perky breasts with tiny tops. Women who wear high heels to work every day. They're all twenty-four, of course, and so can wear high heels all the time because their arches haven't fallen yet."

"Honey. I'm sure—"

"The men who do ask me out figure that, because I'm thirty-two, I'm so desperate that I'll put up with anything."

"No."

"I've had it with men. Sorry, Mom. Forget grandkids."

"Sweetheart, there are plenty of wonderful men out there who don't care about—"

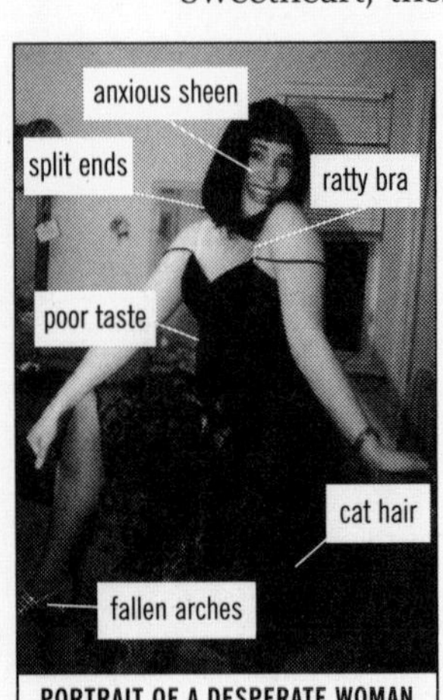

PORTRAIT OF A DESPERATE WOMAN

"No. There aren't. This guy tonight? Awful. We were at his place and he'd made dinner. It was nice—"

"A first date? And you went to his house? Alone?"

"Mom. He's a friend of Cathy's—it's not like he's a mass murderer or anything."

"Still, I don't think that was prudent."

"Mom. It was fine."

"Okay. Go on."

"Honestly, Mom. It was fine. Anyway, we're chatting in his living room and he was nice, I guess, but I wasn't at all attracted to him. Especially after he started complaining of heartburn—from the meal he made, I might add. And what do you say to that? 'Too bad?' 'Want some Tums?'"

"Ella. Have a bit of compassion."

"You're the one who told me never to date a man I pitied."

"You pitied him because he had heartburn? You know, honey, your standards may be a little high."

"I don't know what made me mention it, but I said that when I was a kid I had a heart murmur. Well, this guy leaps up, goes into the bathroom, and comes back with a stethoscope. Before I know it, he has his hand down the front of my shirt."

"What?"

"Here's this guy with heartburn copping a feel as he 'checked it out' and made sure I was 'okay.'"

"Is he a doctor?"

"No. He isn't even a vet. He sells life insurance or computer software or something."

*

CHRISTINE DIDN'T HAVE A CHANCE.

Set up by a mutual friend, Christine (twenty-seven, account manager at an advertising firm) met Todd (twenty-nine, public relations officer at a publishing company) at a party and liked what she saw. A quiet, conservative woman who attends church regularly and never goes on blind dates, Christine leapt at the chance to see Todd again. True, she barely knew him. But Lara had vouched for him: "He's a sweet guy. Outgoing." Good enough.

When Todd called, he suggested a late movie. In turn, Christine suggested that she drive. He agreed. They were set for Saturday night.

Promptly at eight, Christine pulls up in front of Todd's house and prepares to park. She's reversing into a spot when she hears a scream.

"Keep it running!" a man's voice yells.

Christine hesitates over the ignition as she looks up and peers through the window. There, running across the lawn in only a towel, is her date.

"Keep it running!" he repeats.

Todd—sweet, nice, outgoing Todd—hops into the passenger seat and slams the door behind him. In the brief flash of action, Christine gets enough of a view to see that Todd is most definitely naked under that towel.

"Step on it," he gasps. "Drive. I'll explain later. Just *go*!"

A terrible waste of gas.

Alas, Christine never receives an explanation.

They drive around the city for an hour as Todd calms down. She turns up the heat in the car to keep him warm, and they visit a drive-through McDonald's for a burger and fries.

Loathe to ask any questions, Christine bears the awkward silence, which is broken only by Todd's repeated, "It's complicated. I'm sorry." Eventually, she drops him off at home and, as he gets out of the car while holding the towel closed, Todd thanks her. "I'll call you," he says.

I won't answer, thinks Christine as she steps on the gas.

*

JANUARY 3, 10:00 P.M.

Sheila goes to David's house for dinner. This is the big night—wild, animal sex. She is trembling with excitement. David's such a stunning man, and the fact that *he* is making *her* dinner is a thrill. Men never do that for Sheila.

David's gone the whole nine yards—candles, background music, silverware, cloth napkins, spinach wrapped in phyllo pastry as appetizers, delicious pasta with bits of meat and other stuff. There's even raspberry sherbet for dessert.

After dinner, they cuddle on his couch and kiss. It's beautiful. Romantic. Perfect. He has the softest lips, and he uses just the right amount of tongue. Not too wet. Not too dry. Wonderful.

Drawing back to beam at one another, Sheila is hit by a terrible cramp in her stomach. It grumbles and she can feel bile rising. She takes a deep breath to calm the churning and turns to David to tell him that she needs to leave.

"I have something important to tell you," says David. "These past two weeks have been the best. I'm so comfortable and relaxed with you. And I find you incredibly attractive."

Sheila hears the words—*yes, yes, hurry up*—but she can't focus. Her belly is frothing. This only happens when she has an allergic reaction to red wine.

"I think we're really compatible and I know we said we'd take things slow. . . ."

Sheila's mouth fills with that pre–throw up saliva.

"Was there red wine in the pasta sauce?" she says, interrupting David's flow.

"Yes. Listen, I don't want to freak you out. . . ."

Oh no, God no. Not now. She's going to heave.

". . . but I think I'm falling in love with you."

Sheila jumps up, races into his bathroom, and pukes her guts out. The lovely pasta. The three rum and Cokes. The raspberry sherbet. She doesn't even have time to close the door.

Sheila wants to flush herself down the toilet. It's terrible. David comes into the bathroom, holds her hair away from her face, and murmurs sweet things as she purges. When done, Sheila leans back against the tub.

"Was it something I said?" David asks.

*

OLIVIA WAS IN HER THIRTIES when she met a man through a personal ad. An accomplished woman, she wanted to meet someone who had similar values and interests. After talking on the phone a few times, Ian invited Olivia to hear Sallie Tisdale, author of *Talk Dirty to Me*, speak because they both admired her.

SCIATICA
Pain along the sciatic nerve that runs from the lower back down the back of each leg

At first, Olivia was reluctant to attend the event because she wasn't sure there would be a lot of seating in the bar where it was taking place; Olivia has sciatica and can't stand for any length of time. Ian, however, persuaded her that they could meet in the lineup as early as possible to ensure they'd get a seat once the doors opened. He even offered to hold their place in line to give Olivia a break to sit or walk around.

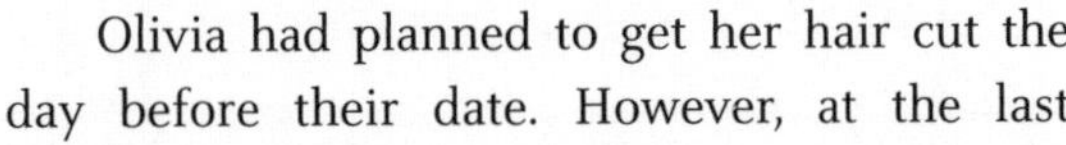

Olivia had planned to get her hair cut the day before their date. However, at the last minute, her hairdresser called to cancel. Olivia quickly booked an appointment with a tony salon she'd never used before—the only available time was about an hour before she was supposed to meet Ian.

Date day. Olivia raced to her appointment. The stylist was very conservative. She left the salon looking like Blanche Deveraux from *The Golden Girls* and headed straight for a public washroom to stick her bouffant under a tap. The poofiness calmed, Olivia started walking to the bar. Halfway there, her stay-ups (which she'd never before worn in public) began to fall down. Ducking into a doughnut shop's washroom, Olivia took them off and then hurried on her way, cold white legs glowing in the November streetlight.

At the venue, Olivia squeezed into yet another tiny washroom cubicle and yanked the stay-ups back on. She then got in line for the event.

Olivia waited alone for almost an hour. During that time, she bumped into three acquaintances: a friend, a former student who hated Olivia because she'd failed her, and a man she'd been in love with for five years (and who'd rebuffed her ungracefully) with his date. All wondered aloud why Olivia was in line waiting to hear the author of *Talk Dirty to Me* by herself.

With no sign of Ian, Olivia was becoming frustrated. A burning sensation ran down her left leg, her foot was getting numb, and the stockings were creeping downward again.

Finally, the crowd was admitted to the room and Olivia grabbed two stools. Trying not to draw too much attention to herself, she massaged her leg. Another half-hour stretched by as she guarded one stool with embarrassment. Finally, only minutes before Tisdale began speaking, Ian stumbled in. He was as high as a kite.

"Sorry I'm late," he mumbled, pupils dilated and a goofy grin on his face. "I got busy with some work and then I looked at the clock and said, 'Wow, it's eight o'clock. Isn't there someplace I was supposed to be?'"

Olivia was fuming.

After the show, Ian offered to buy her a drink at another bar. Once they were settled, he asked if Olivia was angry. "Don't you think your condition is somewhat disrespectful?" asked Olivia, her leg throbbing. "I don't smoke pot any more, though I have many friends who do. It just seems to me like something you do in a different setting."

That was when Ian revealed that selling drugs was how he made his living.

"I have mixed feelings about that," said Olivia, trying to appear accepting and non-judgmental.

There was an awkward pause. Then Ian began berating Olivia for her faults. "Well, you're obviously uptight," he shouted. "Who do you think you are, Ms. Holier than thou. . . ."

Olivia, stiff legged, hobbled out of the bar with Ian hot on her heels. He screamed abuse at her until she, stay-ups now pooled around her ankles, clambered onto a streetcar.

⁂

"OH MY GOD," Tim says, after turning on the bedside light. "There's blood everywhere. Holy shit. Are you okay? Did you get your period?"

Rolling over, Melissa looks down at the sheets. Tim's right. Bright red blood is everywhere. It's even smeared across his stomach.

"Um, I don't think so," she says. "I'm not due for another two weeks."

The young lovers stare at one another for a moment until Tim, blushing and ill at ease, points between her legs. Melissa is shocked—it definitely looks like she has her period.

"We were pretty, uh, energetic," stammers Tim. "Was I too aggressive? Did I hurt you?"

Shaking her head, Melissa examines herself further.

Don't Get Cocky

She and Tim are an item. It's been three months. He caught her eye at a dance club. Tim was, by far, the best dancer in the room: sexy, lean, and moving his hips in ways that reminded Melissa of her tween days spent swooning over John Travolta in *Grease.* He bought her a drink, she made him chuckle over an obscure reference to an old Nana Mouskouri song, and when Melissa had to leave early for another party, both sagged in disappointed.

He called the very next day.

"Tim. I don't think it's me," says Melissa,

returning from the washroom, where she had wiped herself down. "I'm not cut anywhere, and I definitely don't have my period."

To date, Tim and Melissa have had sex forty-two times, and this has never happened before.

"Well, it's not me," says Tim.

"Go wash the blood off and check carefully," says Melissa. "I'll strip the bed."

When Tim disappears into the bathroom, Melissa curses once again the only thing about her boyfriend that she can't stand: he still lives with his parents. *If this were his own place,* she muses, *I could do a load of laundry without waking them or get a glass of water without worrying about the fuck knot in my hair.*

"Holy shit!" Tim shrieks from the bathroom. "Melissa. Call 911. Help. Oh my God. Oh my God!"

"What is it?" she rattles the locked bathroom door. "Open up. Tim? What's going on?"

Melissa hears him moan and say something that sounds like, "I think it's broken."

"Tim?"

Melissa, naked and holding bloody sheets, turns to discover her boyfriend's mother, wrapped in a terry cloth bathrobe, behind her. The older woman barely glances at her as she marches to the bathroom door.

"Honey. What's wrong? Are you okay?"

"Mom, I'm bleeding," Tim answers. "From. . . ."

"Where?" say both mother and girlfriend in unison.

"My, uh, penis."

At this confession, Tim's mother appears to notice for the first time that Melissa is undressed. Melissa is unable to move. She wills her legs to stop trembling.

"Both of you. Get dressed," says his mother. "Tim, wrap your penis in a washcloth to staunch the bleeding and we'll take you to the emergency room."

Somehow, Melissa manages to convince Tim's parents that she can take her boyfriend to the hospital without them.

After an initial examination, Tim and Melissa are ushered into a small room, divided into two sections. Tim sits on the paper laid out by the nurse on the bed, his pants around his ankles and a blood-soaked washcloth protecting his loins.

When the doctor asks Tim if he's comfortable with Melissa remaining in the room, Tim nods. For some reason, a wave of relief washes over her. *He doesn't blame me,* she thinks. *At least, not yet.*

The doctor, a freshly graduated med student, winces in sympathy at the sight of all the blood on Tim's penis. After a few minutes of Tim cringing and yelping and the doctor apologizing, Melissa can't stand it any longer.

"What's wrong with him? Did I hurt him?"

The doctor stands and pulls off his latex gloves. Dropping them into the trash, he makes a note on his clipboard and then turns to address the terrified couple.

"Well, Tim. It appears that you've just lost your virginity, so to speak."

"No. I lost that when I was seventeen."

"What I mean is that you've ruptured your frenulum. That's the membrane that attaches the foreskin to the glans and shaft of the penis. On circumcised men, part of it is usually removed. On uncircumcised men, it can occasionally run the risk of tearing during masturbation or especially vigorous sex."

Both Melissa and Tim turn beet red.

"The good news," continues the doctor, "is that you won't need stitches."

At this news, Tim's face drains of blood. "Thank God," he whispers.

"The bad news is that you two can't have sex for a while. Three weeks, maybe a month. Nothing—no hand jobs or oral sex, either."

It's Melissa's turn go faint.

'tis true that we are in great danger;
The greater therefore should our courage be.

WILLIAM SHAKESPEARE, *Henry V*

eleven

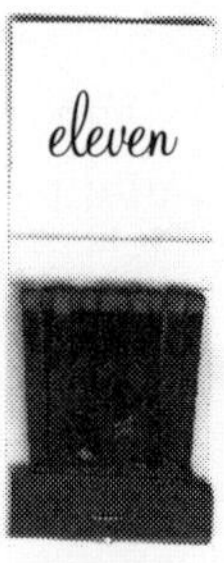

Holy-Shit Moments

"AMY? IT'S WES. I know you're there. I can see you walking around your apartment. Pick up the phone."

It's 1:30 a.m. and Wesley is speaking into my answering machine, one of those old clanky contraptions that plays the message aloud as it's being recorded.

"I can see you standing there. Let me in."

Wesley and I work together. Six months earlier, I moved to this city for my new job. Out of my depth and away from friends, I was terribly lonely. During the day, I fumbled through various assignments, my heart racing and hands shaking. My body was on high alert from nine in the morning until seven or so at night, at which point I'd come home, feed the cats, and watch TV for five hours until I fell asleep.

For six months, Wesley kept quiet about his crush on me. When he finally told me about it, I experienced a moment of weakness. He's nice, I told myself. He's sort of cute. Okay, with the right clothes and haircut he might be cute. I'm lonely.

I'm bored of my own company. I want to kiss someone.

I made a terrible mistake and kissed Wesley.

"Amy. Pick up the goddamn phone. I can see you standing there, listening to me. Just pick it up. Better yet, let me in. We need to talk."

Almost as soon as my lips first touched his, I knew that I was in trouble. Tears filled Wesley's eyes and he clutched me to him. I thought I heard him whisper that he loved me. I *know* I heard him say, "Never leave me."

I did care about him. He was my first friend in this godforsaken city. He'd helped me innumerable times with the stories I was assigned to write for the provincial newspaper. He was kind and generous. He'd made me laugh on a daily basis and was the only person in that town to hug me when my beloved grandmother died.

I just wasn't attracted to him. He had a slightly manic look—an hours-spent-in-a-dark-basement-reading-medieval-porn kind of look. Lacking in confidence, Wesley was the type to heartily agree with anything I said. This drove me nuts, considering I know that, most of the time, at least, I'm wrong.

But I kissed him.

And now he is stalking me.

"Where've you been all night? I called and called and you didn't pick up. I drove by earlier and your lights were all off. Where did you go? Are you seeing someone else? Let me *in*!"

In truth, I'd been fast asleep. I had big plans for Saturday afternoon (go to Wal-Mart and buy supplies, see a movie, bring my car in for a tune-up and maybe a shampoo) but was so depressed by my to-do list, I went to bed. I had woken up an hour before this lunatic called and was making myself some supper.

I suppose I hadn't left things well with Wes. A couple of days after our kiss, I took him out for coffee and explained that I was just getting over someone (sort of true—I was over him already, but Wes didn't need to know that) and that though he was a really excellent, super, and eligible man, he and I were not made for one another. He didn't take it well. He cried. I wanted to crawl beneath the table but instead I hugged him, paid the bill, and left.

Now he's outside my apartment. Calling me from his car phone and watching me listen to his message. This is beyond creepy.

BEEP!

Hallelujah! The machine cuts him off, and I walk into the back room to call my sister and tell her what just happened. I'm just switching on the light when the phone rings again. Oh, God. It's him.

"Amy? Where did you go? In the back room? Oh, yeah. I can see the light. Will you please pick up? Pick up the phone. We need to talk. I need to talk. Don't just stand there. I can see you listening. I know you're listening. Let me in. Or pick up the goddamn phone!"

Amy,
I have walked among the insane and I am one of them. They accepted me and accepted them.
I would like you to accept these gifts and me.

[One of the scarier love letters I've received]

Okay, he's scaring me now. What do I do? How do I get this madman to go away?

I drop to the floor.

"Oh, that's mature. What? You're going to belly crawl through the apartment now? Really adult of you, Amy. Now, get the fuck up and pick up the phone."

I drag myself along the carpeted hallway until I reach the inside door that leads to the third-floor apartment. I barely know the woman who lives upstairs, but I'm so freaked out I don't know what else to do. I hear classical music through the door. Thank God. She's home.

I bang on the door and call her name.

"Diane. Can you hear me? Can you unlock your side, please? I need help."

The music stops and footsteps pound down the stairs. I hear the click of the lock and the door swings open, nearly clipping me on the forehead.

"What are you doing?" Diane's upside-down face stares at me. I explain the situation from my position prone on the floor.

Diane works at an abused women's safe house downtown and has little needlepoint cushions around her apartment displaying famous feminist quotations by women like Betty Friedan ("It is easier to live through someone else than to become complete yourself") and Faith Whittlesey ("Ginger Rogers did everything Fred Astaire did, but she did it backwards and in high heels"). Clearly, I've come to the right person.

Diane marches into my apartment, holding a middle finger aloft toward the windows. She yanks the phone cord out of the wall and grabs a huge sheet of bristol board. *Am calling cops,* she writes in enormous grape-smelling Crayola letters. *Asshole,* she adds, for good measure, at the bottom.

Holding it against her chest, Diane walks from window to window with the sign and a cordless phone tucked beneath her ear. I crawl around on the floor behind her. After two minutes, we hear a car start up and roar off into the night. Diane, who was actually ordering a pizza on the phone, looks at me and the tension breaks. We both start laughing and crying.

The next day, there is a needlepoint pillow tucked inside the door I share with Diane. I'm reeling from the news that Wes resigned that morning and is moving to another city. But, as I read the pillow—"I am woman. I am strong. I am very, very tired"—I realize that I've made my first girlfriend in this city.

*

REMEMBER THE X FACTOR? The unpredictable twist that turns your dream date into *The Rocky Horror Picture Show*?

It's as though the goddesses are bored up there, lounging around in their golden palaces in the clouds, eating bonbons delivered by hunky angels, and they decide to screw with you just for the hell of it.

Dating is inherently scary. It takes a lot of courage to open yourself up to someone, reveal things to a near-stranger. You don't know each other's emotional triggers yet, so anything you say can potentially set the other person off. When this happens, it's quite frightening. These are the moments when you wish for bodyguards, your big brother, or, best of all, your father with his shotgun. These are the moments when you offer your soul to the devil simply to escape. The moments when all you can say is "holy shit."

❋

JULY 14, 10:59 P.M. A KITCHEN.

I don't know about this guy. He's so . . . changeable. The first time we met he was charming and hilarious. The second time, sullen and depressed (granted, his art gallery had received a nasty review in the paper that morning). The third time he had me laughing like a maniac and now, tonight, he's all serious and sober. I don't understand it.

At dinner, he asked me all about my parents and brothers. He wanted to know details about the pets I had while growing up and how I managed to scrape together the financing for the flower shop. It was a conversation about me, which I'd normally be all over, but even though he was asking the right questions, he was distracted. He ordered the same bottle of wine twice and when the second one came, he sent it back. He salted his meal about six times and asked me to remind him whether I had a brother or a sister after I'd just finished talking about being the only girl in a family of four boys.

"What's wrong with you?" I blurted.

Adam laughed and apologized. "Preoccupied with shit I've got to do for the opening tomorrow night. Actually, you can help if you want."

It's kind of sweet. Adam asked me back to his place so we could continue the date while he finished stuff up for work. He's offered me a drink and I figure we'll start packaging art to bring to the gallery or something like that.

* * *

11:09 p.m.

We're baking. At least, that's what I think we're doing. Adam's just pulled out a bunch of cookie sheets. Strange. I've never been to an art opening before, but I thought galleries would find homemade cookies less than chic. Or maybe that's the point. . . .

* * *

11:11 p.m.

Holy. Shit. I've got to figure out a way to get out of here. Oh my God. Oh. God. What do I say? How do I say no?

* * *

12:30 a.m.

I'm free. I'm *free*!

I'm naive. I'm pathetic. I deal with flowers all day long—they're simple. Easy. Beautiful. Not demanding. No awkward questions. I'm sticking with flowers. Forget men.

Adam pulled out the baking sheets and I automatically thought *chocolate chip cookies.*

Instead, he reached into the cupboard underneath the sink and produced a large bottle of ammonia and a bag of what looked like flour.

"Ever made crack before?" he asked.

"Ever made what before?"

"Crack."

"Crack what?"

"Crack cocaine."

"Um, no." I watched as he sifted what I can only assume was coke onto the baking sheet.

"It's pretty simple, really," he said, fiddling with a box of baking soda. "You have to let it sit overnight. Well, it's better that way. So that's why I want to get it done tonight, in time for tomorrow's opening."

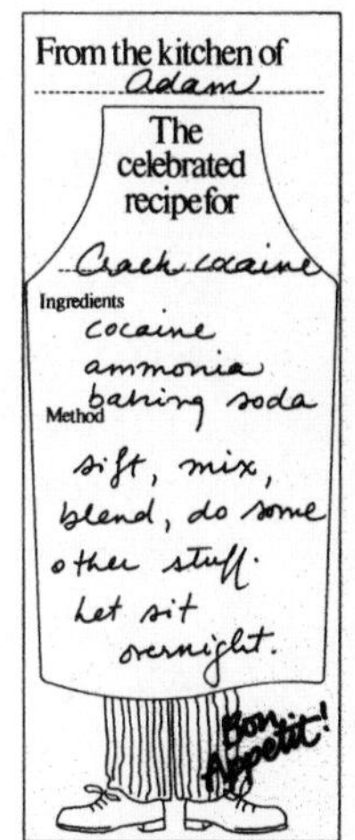

I couldn't help myself. "What, you hand out crack at the door?"

"No, no," he laughed, smiling at me with an engaging, warm grin. "It's for my artists. And very special patrons. The ones who spend a load of dough." He winked and turned back to his work.

I got out of there the only way I knew how—I excused myself to the bathroom, tapped my foot for five minutes, and then returned to the kitchen to announce that my period had just arrived and I needed my cramp pills, which, of course, were at home.

"Thanks for the . . . night," I said, racing off into the pitch-black yard. It's the first time I'd ever embraced being alone in the dark on an unknown street.

"WHY ARE YOU BUGGING ME about this?" huffs Lola. "For the last time, I adore Mike. I won't hurt Mike. I love Mike. Now will you get off my back?"

Vicky drops her end of the barbecue and places her hands

on her hips. Cocking her head to one side, she watches as Lola collapses on the ground.

"Vic. I swear. I won't hurt him." Lola shades her eyes from the sun to look at her friend. "I know he's your brother. I promise I won't be mean. I promise I'll support him and encourage him and love him and feed him chicken soup when he's sick. Okay?"

Vicky sighs. "He's been hurt in the past and I just don't want him to go through another bad relationship. His last girlfriend was, well, abusive. She yelled and screamed at him if he forgot to pick up milk or tampons. She even swatted him once. I just want you to be nice to him."

"For Chrissakes, Vic. I'm not going to *hit* him. I might yell once in a while when we're arguing, but I'm not abusive. And he's dear and wonderful and I know that he's been hurt. I'm going to try everything I can do to make this work."

"Okay. I'm sorry. I'm just worried about him, that's all." Vicky rises. "Now, help me with this damn thing. People will be arriving any second."

If I didn't like Mike so much, Lola muses as she hefts the barbecue once more, *I'd break up with him just because of his bloody sister.*

It's Lola's thirtieth birthday and Vicky insisted on celebrating by planning a huge barbecue for their group of friends. Three hours earlier, Vicky called Lola over. "I need your help," she said, "and I want to talk to you about something before everyone gets here."

Lola had known that this talk was coming. Ever since she started dating Mike—after meeting him at Vicky's engagement party—Lola could tell her friend was pissed. And she *had* broken Rule #2 in the friend's handbook: Don't date their siblings. (Rule #1 is: Don't date their ex-boyfriends.)

Lola tossed Rule #2 out the window as soon as she laid eyes

on brawny, tanned Mike. At the party, he sidled over to her, enveloped her in a hug, and said, "So I finally meet the woman who keeps getting my sister into trouble. Who are you going to play with now that she's met her match?"

"You."

Lola really did say that. Her boldness seemed to work. They went back to his place that night and have only spent two days apart since.

The sound of a large engine interrupts the lazy chirping of birds, and Lola runs toward the driveway.

"Dammit!" calls Vicky. "Come back here!"

Lola arrives just in time to see Mike sliding off his motorcycle. He pulls off his helmet.

"Hi, gorgeous," he says as he swoops her into a deep kiss.

It's going to be a great birthday.

The party rages for six hours. Friends smother Lola with gifts and helium balloons. Mike keeps bringing her more drinks. And Lola can't help but get some satisfaction by listening to Vicky swear over the heat of the ancient, rusty barbecue.

Late into the evening, Mike and Lola head to the front of the house.

"Wait!" calls Vicky. "You're leaving? But it's your party."

"I am, I know, and thank you so much." Lola wraps her arms around her friend and then turns to Mike's motorcycle. "It's been the best birthday, and it's about to get better." She leers at Mike and pulls on her helmet while Vicky pretends to retch.

Mike starts the motorcycle as Vicky calls out to Lola: "Remember what we talked about earlier! You've promised me!"

"Don't worry," answers Lola, performing an elaborate pirouette while throwing her leg over the seat. "I won't do anything to hurt—"

She kicks Mike in the head. He falls off the bike.

"Shit."

Avert misunderstanding by calm, poise and balance.

❄

TANYA KNEW THAT GEORGE WAS going to be at the party. What she didn't expect was a weakness in the knees, her heart skipping a beat, and her palms immediately becoming sweaty. *What is wrong with me?* she wondered. *We broke up eight months ago. I should be over him by now. Damn. I hope he can't see me shaking.*

Two years ago, George marched over to Tanya in a 7-Eleven, where she was reading fashion magazines she couldn't afford to buy, and asked her out. Something about his long, thick eyelashes and confident posture made her say yes. For a year, they were happy together. George was goofy, silly, and, after a few drinks, bordered on wild. Tanya, who was rather reserved most of the time, felt freed by him. She could say or do anything and George would just go with the flow.

However, the last four months of their relationship were awful. George started hanging out with a crowd that included a number of tasty young things with doe eyes and long legs. Tanya was never sure whether he actually cheated on her, but he certainly didn't make her feel secure. When she was accepted into a master's program, George was less than supportive. With the glow of the "honeymoon period" gone and nothing solid to back it up, their relationship fizzled.

This was the first time they'd seen each other since the breakup. Tanya knew, from a mutual friend, that he'd dated someone briefly and was now single again. *Dangerous territory,* she thought. *I'm single, lonely, and the sex with George was superb. Better to stay far, far away.*

Ducking into various rooms and hiding behind sofas, Tanya managed to avoid direct contact with George until he stood by the pool and bellowed her name. Everyone stopped. He waited. Sheepish, Tanya finally stepped out from behind a potted palm on the terrace and George started clapping. *Damn. He can still make me laugh even when he's embarrassing me.*

"What do you want?" she hissed at him while partygoers—having no clue as to what was going on, but sensing a dramatic moment—cheered as she made her way over to him.

"You. I've missed you." He wrapped his arms around her waist and swung her into the air. "I want you back. And I'm going to prove my love for you tonight. Come with me."

Tanya was too surprised to do anything but allow herself to be dragged to his car.

"But . . . I . . ." she stuttered.

"No buts. And I know you're not seeing anyone right now. You came to the party alone." A wolfish grin consumed his face. "I checked."

As he roared out of the parking spot, George fiddled with the knob of the stereo, settling on an old country station. He turned it up so loud that Tanya couldn't hear any of the sounds coming from his mouth even though he continued to talk.

"WHERE ARE WE GOING?" she yelled.

"TO THAT MAGICAL PLACE WHERE I FIRST LAID EYES ON YOU," screamed George.

"ARE YOU HIGH?" Tanya screeched.

"NO. ARE YOU?"

Tanya fell back into her seat, dazed.

Sure enough, ten minutes later, George pulled into the parking lot of the 7-Eleven. She started to pull on the door handle to get out, but George stopped her. "Wait here," he said, hopping out of the car. "I'll just be a minute."

Thirty seconds later, George raced out of the store and threw himself into the car. Tires squealing, he veered onto the street.

"What are you doing?" Tanya asked.

"I've got a present for you," he said, rummaging inside his coat. "Here." He handed her the current issue of the fashion magazine she'd been perusing two years ago. "Oh, look. There's another one."

George pulled into the lot of another 7-Eleven. Again, he left the car running and got out before Tanya could ask what the hell he was up to. Watching him through the plate-glass windows, Tanya was confused. *What is going on with him?* George wandered through the aisles and then shrugged with dramatic flair. Moments later, he sauntered out the door.

"Hold out your hands," he said. Tanya put her hands out before him and he released fistfuls of gummy bears, Swedish berries, and bottle caps. "Voila!"

As he roared out of the parking lot, Tanya asked, "Are you shoplifting?"

"We're on a crime spree," he said, gunning it down the street. "I'm taking you on a crime spree. We're like Bonnie and Clyde. Kermit and Miss Piggy. P. Diddy and J.Lo."

"You're insane," Tanya couldn't help but point out. "Kermit and Miss Piggy were Muppets, and good Muppets for that matter. And P. Diddy and J.Lo broke up, like, years ago."

"What does it matter? I love you and I'm showing you how much by stealing for you. Aha, another one," George swerved into yet another 7-Eleven parking lot. "Be right back."

"George. No," Tanya said, but he was already gone. "Asshole. Idiot. Twit. Jerk. Freak."

Moments later he came racing out of the store, screaming, "Step on it! Pedal to the metal, baby!"

Later, Tanya wouldn't remember leaping over the gearshift, but suddenly she was in the driver's seat, backing the car out of their spot. George grabbed the passenger door and scrambled inside as an irate 7-Eleven manager ran after him.

"Sorry, T. All I could get was this." He tossed a package of diapers onto her lap.

She drove herself home.

*

JULY 7, 1962.

How quickly can a girl's reputation be ruined?

Pete told Caelah's parents that he was taking her to a late movie. Instead, they drove up to Beaver Lake on the mountain.

Parked cars filled all of the usual spots at the lookout, so they circled around and found a secluded spot on the other side of the lake. It was so lovely. The moon was reflected in the water and the air was warm and soft.

Pete kept the car battery on so they could listen to music. Then he got out of the car. Caelah thought he was taking a piss, but when he crawled into the back seat he was naked.

Not wanting to be a prude—besides, he was kissing her neck in that way that made her want to scream—Caelah took off her shirt. This then turned into a cramped striptease. Pete loved it. Especially when she twirled her underwear around her finger.

Pete had just rolled on a condom and was about to put it in when someone knocked on the car window.

A cop was shining his flashlight into the sedan. His light wavered on Caelah's boobs for a few seconds too long, and then he made that "roll down your window" motion to Pete. He started his interrogation.

They sat there, not a stitch of clothing on, and as Caelah answered every question, she felt her reputation nose-dive. "Where do you live?" Her parents will find out. "How old are you?" Old enough to know better. "What school do you go to?" Friends and teachers will whisper in the halls. "Do you know this man?" She's a shameless hussy, no better than a streetwalker.

If her parents ever find out what happened tonight, life as Caelah knows it will be over. Her father will lock her up and her mother will marry her off to that nerdy, pimply faced creep at church who's two years younger than her. It won't matter that Pete is an upperclassman or that his parents are in the same social circle as hers.

Cowering behind Pete, one hand over her genitals and the other over her breasts, Caelah knew one thing for sure: Her days as a good girl are over.

❄

FROM: Sharon
DATE: Thursday, October 7, 2003 2:37PM
TO: Amy
SUBJECT: A man I should never have dated . . .

I was seeing this guy for a month. Maybe a month. Probably more like three weeks. Things intensified very quickly. We were mad about each other and I think we were already using the "L" word.

We made plans to meet after I got off work (he doesn't work—pretty well never has and, as it turns out, never will). Our big date would begin at his musty, stained hovel, move to dinner at a new Chinese restaurant (I would pay, of course), and then end back at my place.

When I arrived on his street, I saw him being frogmarched away by a police officer. Three cop cars were parked haphazardly on his front lawn, and neighbours hunched on doorsteps to watch.

I ran up to him, full of questions, but the cop shoved him into the back seat of a car and wouldn't let me talk to him. Indignant, I demanded answers. Once they found out I'm the girlfriend, they rolled their eyes and one of them explained that he had been arrested for stealing some photos and other objects of sentimental value from his ex-girlfriend. Apparently, it was all part of a blackmail scheme to get him access to his unofficial six-year-old stepdaughter.

He spent the evening at 52 Division.

I stayed at home, vowing to stand by my man.

And I did. Despite the arrest and many, many other inauspicious signs, I stayed with the guy—for another, oh, five years.

❋

SEPTEMBER 3.

"Louise, it's me."

"Becca. So you got home safely?"

"Yes. No problems. I hate long bus rides, but this one was just fine."

"Why? What's going on?"

"I met someone."

"On the bus?"

"Yes. And he's adorable. He was sitting in the seat behind me and kept glancing over my shoulder to see what I was reading."

"That would annoy the hell out of me."

"No it wouldn't. Not when the guy looks like Hugh Jackman."

"Really?"

"Truly. His name is Ted and he's sooooo cute. Gorgy-porgy."

"So you talked?"

"Oh, we did more than that."

"Skank. On a bus?"

"Get your mind out of the gutter. We didn't have sex, but we made out like crazy on the back seat. Don't worry, the bus was pretty empty."

"Are you going to see him again?"

"Yeah. He lives in Harding, which is a pain, but what's an hour's drive for a steamy, molten hunk of sex? And he asked for my address. He said he'd write me. Sigh."

"I can't believe it. You're here for a week, pick up four guys and one on the bus, and I can't get a date to my sister's wedding."

"Honey. My pheromones are just pumping—this always happens to me in the fall."

"You are so strange."

"Well, I wanted to thank you again for hosting me, lovely Lou. It was a blast."

"Any time, Becca. Maybe you can bring your new dreamboat up with you next time you come."

"Oh, I'll come with him any time."

"You really are a skank."

* * *

September 7.

"Becca! I'm glad I caught you—I'm running out to a party but I wanted to know, what's the name of that store we went into the other day? The one off the alley?"

"I don't think. . . . Wasn't it Marylou's? Or Marrywhosit Whosit?"

"Merry Frou Frou's. That's it. I knew you'd remember. I'm going to run over there and get a birthday gift."

"Whose birthday?"

"Dave's. Hey, did you hear from your molten sex god?"

"No. Fucker."

"I'm sorry about that. I've got to run, though. Talk later?"

"You bet."

* * *

September 30.

"Lou? Oh, thank God. You have to help me. You won't believe what happened."

"You okay? You sound frazzled or freaked out or something."

"I'm freaking out. I'm fucking frazzled, freaked out, *and* frantic. I just got a letter from Ted."

"Who?"

"The Hugh Jackman look-alike. Sex god. Remember? The bus dude?"

"Oh. You got a letter? It's about bloody time."

"You don't understand. It was a letter from prison."

"What?"

"Prison. The big house. The slammer. Jail. The penal complex. Pokey—"

"Okay. I get it. Slow down. Breathe. Tell me what it says."

"'Dear Rebecca, I'm sorry I haven't written or called sooner but some stuff came up since I last saw you . . .'"

"I'll say."

"Let me read it. My God, my hands are shaking. Okay. '. . . Since I last saw you. I didn't tell you this on the bus because I knew you wouldn't talk to me. No one wants to date a guy who is in jail. Even though I'm innocent. I was incarcerated six months ago for assault and I was on day parole for good behaviour when we met. I just couldn't stand it any more. I had to get out of there. You can't know what it's like to be locked up and not able to leave. It's awful. Anyway, I don't know why I thought I could get away with it, but I went down to the bus station and got on the first bus. I believe it was meant to be, because I met you. Thinking of you is the only thing that's keeping me sane in here. Because I broke my parole, the judge has tacked on another six months to my sentence.'"

Thinking of You

With good behaviour, Ted might get out in a year and a half. It took Becca only a month and a half to move to a new address.

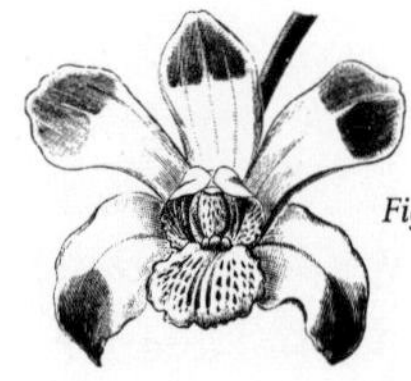

Fig. 1 Orchidacea, Chysis chelsoni

A very important form of fear that many [men] have is not the fear of a woman's body, but of her sexual organ—the vagina. Even touching it causes certain men to shudder. They feel that great harm may come to them if they do.

EDWIN W. HIRSCH, *The Power to Love*, 1934

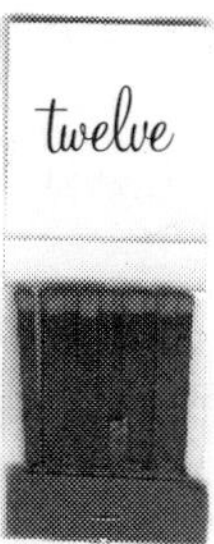

Men Who Shouldn't Date. Ever.

I'VE STARTED OFF THE LAST ELEVEN CHAPTERS with the story of one of my own bad dates that relates to the subject at hand. I'm pleased to say that, when it comes to the topic of this particular chapter, I've never had a date like any of these women.

I was going to put "Men Who Shouldn't Date" at the beginning of the book—a hook of unbelievable stories that would lure you into reading the rest. However, the problem was just that: these stories are unbelievable. There was no way, dear Reader, you'd believe they were true if you hadn't read the rest of the book first. And so, without further ado, I give you some of the most outrageous, the strangest—hell, the worst—dates I've ever heard.

*

THE PHONE CALL—short, to the point, mind-boggling—comes out of the blue.

"Pam? It's Elliot. I've missed you. Can we meet up this weekend?"

Pam is astounded. She hasn't heard from her ex in a year and a half. Not that she wanted to—their breakup was long and painful. By the time he'd removed all of his boxers, shaving cream, and navy blue socks from her home, Pam was ready to kill him.

"Um. Elliot. Wow," she hedges. "How are you?"

"I need to see you. I promise it won't take longer than an hour. There's some stuff I feel I should have said and never did."

Despite frantic, high-alert, deafening warning bells—hang up! don't say yes! don't get sucked in! remember, charm is his weapon!—Pam is intrigued. This is a man who never wanted to talk about their relationship—factor one in their breakup. Factor two: the amount of time he spent at work. Factor three: he was boring, unromantic, staid, and by the book. The very same reasons why Elliot is a rising star at a high-powered liberal law firm.

"Okay," says Pam, regretting it instantly. "Saturday night. Eight o'clock. One hour. Then I have plans."

"Perfect. Thank you," says Elliot. "I really have missed you."

"Whatever." Annoyed, Pam just wants to hang up. "Bye."

"Bye, Mellow." Shit. He used his sweet name for her. He only used that when he was trying to get laid. Shit, shit, damn.

On Saturday afternoon, Pam denies that she's cleaning her home for Elliot's visit. In fact, just to prove how little she cares about this man, she won't change her bedsheets no matter how badly they need to be washed. And there's no way she's washing the floors for him. She does clean the toilet, though. She doesn't want him to think she turned into a slob after they broke up.

Pam isn't sure why she's having this reaction to Elliot's visit. It's not like she wants him back.

At eight on the nose, the doorbell rings. Pam, standing in the hallway, counts ten steamboats before answering the door.

"Hello, Mellow." Elliot kisses her on the cheek.

A surge of relief floods through Pam. She feels . . . nothing. Even the Hugo Boss cologne that used to make her eyes roll back in her head is doing nothing for her.

"Hi, Elliot." Motioning for him to come in, Pam closes the door and resolves to move the conversation along. If she plays her cards right, she might be sipping her first Granny Apple martini with Anna by 9:15 p.m.

"A drink?" she asks.

"Please. A beer would be great."

"So what did you want to talk about?" Pam says, walking to the kitchen.

"I'll wait until we're settled," Elliot yells from the living room. "No rush."

To hell with that, thinks Pam. She grabs a bottle of cold beer from the fridge door and eschews offering him a glass in favour of speeding things along. She pours herself a glass of chilled white wine and balances a bowl of nuts in the crook of one elbow.

"So, how's work . . ." Pam starts to ask. What? The lights are off. Candles are flickering. What is going on?

A movement in the corner of the room, near the stereo, catches her eye, and she turns. Pam hears the strains of Nina Simone's "My Baby Just Cares for Me" as Elliot steps from the shadows. He's naked. Not even wearing his watch. The bowl of nuts falls to the ground and shatters.

As Elliot steps toward her, his hand working his cock, Pam is reminded of why she dated him. He's hung like Secretariat.

"Elliot," she says. "What the fuck are you doing?"

"I've missed you. I can't stop thinking about you. Naked. Beneath me."

"Oh, for God's sake. I'm not interested. We haven't seen each other—"

The doorbell rings. Could it be that a Jehovah's Witness will save her? "Put your clothes on."

Pam is ready to throw her arms around whoever is selling, whatever they're selling, but is surprised to see a young, pretty woman at her door, a baby on her hip.

"Can I help you?"

"You fucking slut!" the woman screams. "You goddamn home wrecker. You should be ashamed of yourself." Pushing past Pam, the woman wheels into the living room and yells, "I fucking knew it!" The baby starts to cry.

"Um, what's going on here? Who are you?" asks Pam.

"I'm his fucking wife." The woman points to Elliot, who's scrambling to pull on his boxers. "And this is his fucking baby. And you're his fucking whore."

Pam trots out every line she can think of to calm this woman down. "I haven't seen Elliot in a year and a half. I didn't even know he was married. Obviously, you two have some things to work out so why don't you go home. . . ."

"I'm his fucking wife!

"You told me you weren't having an affair." The woman bursts into tears, hands the baby to Pam, and collapses on the couch, sobbing. "You l-l-lied t-t-to m-m-me."

Elliot, shirtless but deflated cock tucked back in pants at least, races over to comfort his wife. "Manya, shhh." He holds her. "I didn't lie. Nothing's happened between me and Pam. I'm not even attracted to her. I was just so mad at you. . . ."

Pam doesn't want to listen to this crap, and the squirming baby is now screaming in her arms. "Excuse me. Can the baby have some juice?" she asks.

Elliot nods without stopping. ". . . You weren't listening to me and so I figured if you're treating me like I'm having an affair, I might as well. . . ."

Pam enters the kitchen and starts to coo to the baby. *How did I get into this mess? I don't even know the baby's name. I don't even know if it's a boy or a girl.* Rummaging through the fridge, she finds an apple juice box for the baby and pours herself a shot of vodka.

Two hours later, Manya, Elliot, and their baby (a girl named Patricia) finally leave. Pam, who had, on average, a vodka shot for every new bout of screaming that came from the living room and can't count her own fingers, doesn't bother to see them out. Elliot and Manya never apologize.

AUGUST 10, 11:13 P.M.

It should have been a perfect night. I liked him. He liked me. We'd been out on two wonderful dates and tonight should have been full of romance and possibility and tension. Lovely, sweet sexual tension.

Instead, I never want to date again. I don't care if I die old, lonely, and sad. I hate men.

A soft, cool breeze is in the air tonight, and so when Rob suggested a midnight canoodle on the beach after dinner, I was in heaven. Here's a guy who really *does* like long strolls on the beach. We grabbed an old wool blanket and a bottle of wine for later and then hopped into his car.

At first, I didn't notice what he was doing. I was chattering away about the overprotective parent that wanted her two children in my daycare to eat separately from the rest of the kids so as not to pick up their "bad eating habits and disgusting manners." When I glanced at him to see if he found this as funny as I did, he was staring out the window, not even watching the road. I figured something unusual—a cool car, a neat skateboard trick, a new store—had caught his eye and carried on.

Then he started barking.

Alarmed, I looked over at my date. He was staring at the hookers lining the street. As that tidbit of information was sinking in, I also realized that we were well off the route to the Thai restaurant we'd chosen for dinner. He'd *chosen* to drive along Richards Street in order to see the prostitutes. He'd done this on purpose.

Hi. I'm a pig.

"Oh, yeah, baby," he said, hanging out of the window. "Show me more of that. Arrrowrrow!" he howled.

"Rob! What are you doing?" I was sickened.

He ignored me and continued screaming at all the women we passed.

"How much for a blow job, sugar?"

"A little black pussy? Meow!"

"Turn that sweet ass around. Shake what your mama gave you."

"Grrrr. You a tiger, baby? A bad, wild tiger?"

My stomach was heaving.

When he pulled up at a stoplight, I got out of the car.

"Hey, where are you going?"

"You disgust me." I was shaking with rage.

"Whaaa? They like it. That's why they're out here."

"No, you pig. They are out here because they need money to feed drug habits and the scared little kids at home in nasty apartments that they share with four other women."

I hailed a cab and came home, leaving the lovely wool blanket that my aunt gave me in the fucker's car.

❋

SATURDAY NIGHT, 6:50 P.M.

The subway is taking forever. I'm supposed to be at Eglinton station in ten minutes. I've been standing here waiting for at least fifteen. I'm definitely going to be late. Not that that would be such a bad thing. I don't know why I agreed to this blind date, anyway.

Marilyn assured me that Joseph is a "lovely, dear man," but coming from a fifty-eight-year-old married co-worker, I don't know how much to trust her. I mean, sure, he and I talked on the phone, but there were some discrepancies.

For example, Marilyn said Joseph is a chef. He admitted that he's only in his first year of cooking school. She said he's always wanted to be a chef. Joseph told me that this is a stop-gap measure to get his parents off his back. Marilyn told me he's living at home because he's saving to buy a house. He told me that he hasn't thought about buying a house; he just needs to save money.

I've got to give this guy a chance. He seems nice enough. A little uncomfortable but, then again, so was I. And he's coming in all the way from Hamilton to meet me. Though that's another problem. I don't want a long-distance relationship—even if it is only an hour's drive.

I hope he recognizes me. I told him I'd wear my red coat, but if I'm late he may have to ask a bunch of women wearing red if they're Rachel.

Finally: the subway.

* * *

6:59 p.m.

Okay. Just be calm. The subway is pulling into the station. Don't be nervous. Wipe hands on coat just in case he wants to shake them.

I can't see him yet. He said he's tall with straight brown hair that flops into his eyes. About 180 pounds. Okay. . . . Nope. Don't see. . . .

Oh. My. God. That can't be him. Oh, no. Quick, take off coat. Hide coat. Oh, no. Shit. Why did I tell him what I would be wearing? He sees me. Oh, shit shit shit. No, no, no. He's hideous. And if he's "tall," then I'm Pamela Anderson. Holy fuck. He's got to weigh at least 240 pounds. And he's covered in acne. Oh, no. Here he comes.

* * *

7:02 p.m.

He has a twitch. A tic. He has a weird fucking spasm that jerks his left shoulder up to his left ear. And then he flaps his earlobe twice with his thumb. Oh, God. I'm so shallow.

* * *

7:05 p.m.

He can't be serious. He can't be telling me this. Did he really just say that he beat a homeless man with his shoe because "the dirtbag" asked him for change? No. This can't be happening. He beat up a homeless guy?

* * *

7:08 p.m.

I've *got* to get off this subway. He just described beating this man—no more than twenty minutes ago—and leaving him "whimpering" on the floor of the bus shelter. Holy crap. Where were the cops to arrest this asshole? I've got to get away from him. *Now.*

* * *

7:10 p.m.

I'm free! I'm free! The subway just pulled into St. Clair station. He said, "I don't know how anyone lives in the Big Smoke with all the bums. How does a pretty little gal like you deal with them?" And I fucking bolted. Just as the doors were about to close, I said, "Joseph, I totally forgot. I've got to go," and I hustled my ass out of there.

Hailing a cab. Going home. Never talking to Marilyn again.

*

FROM: Marianne
DATE: Thursday, June 17, 2004 4:00PM
TO: Amy
SUBJECT: And I still have his number . . . if you're interested

I met Philip at a friend's office Christmas party. He was in the creative side of the ad company—the ones who have figurines on their desks with stacks of comic books and a foosball table nearby.

I liked him immediately because he was so irreverent. He had no interest in social norms—at one point, he leapt onto a table and danced like a fiend to Prince's "I Wanna Be Your Lover." He did it so unself-consciously that I was fascinated. Full of confidence and creativity, he used some wrapping paper to fold an origami swan for me. He made me laugh and I adored him.

We went out a few times and had a blast. On our first date, he took me to a Dungeons and Dragons tournament—I didn't know people still played that—where we were admitted as "spectators." It was insane, and yet somehow it was also fun.

We dated for about six weeks. We always saw each other late at night—he was not much of a day person, so started work after lunch and worked through dinner. Our dates generally started at ten or eleven at night.

One night, after Philip had been away for a four-day meeting in another city, he showed up at my door.

I welcomed him with a hug and tried to kiss him but he swivelled his head away. He refused to say anything and I was wondering what the hell was going on when he covered his mouth with one hand and said, "I want to show you something."

"Okay."

"I didn't go away like I said."

"Okay." I was totally confused.

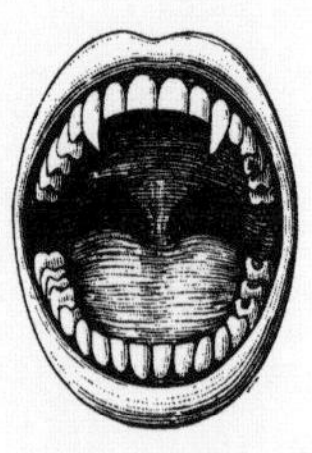

Fangs would have been her third choice

"I went to the dentist and got these." He pulled his hand away to reveal . . . *fangs!*

He'd had his canine teeth replaced with fangs that dipped about half an inch below his other teeth.

Maybe he was going for the Jackalwere or Beholder look, but if he was going to take D&D role-playing to such an extreme, I would've preferred a Sorcerer or even a Halfling Monk.

❋

LAURA IS A PETITE BLONDE who works in a designer clothing store for women. Rod is strapping, a former rugby player with midnight-black hair. They look fabulous together.

When Rod sidles up to Laura in a bar, her friends are agog with the pure physical beauty of the match. He's smarter than he looks. So is she. They agree to have dinner later in the week.

On their first date, Laura is seriously crushing on Rod. She can't get over how generous and sensitive he seems. He's a little cocky, but she kind of likes a bit of that in a man. She agrees to a second date.

A week later, Laura walks to the address Rod has given her over the phone. It's an enormous stone house with a beautiful wildflower garden in the front. He's only thirty-five and he owns this? Very cool.

It's his parents' house, Rod explains when she compliments him on the garden. He still lives at home but his parents are out for the night, and so he wanted to cook her dinner. He hands her a glass of wine and takes her on a tour. On his bedroom wall are posters of AC/DC and the Clash. She's disappointed.

Over the dinner he's prepared—pasta a little too soggy and salad a lot too vinegary—Laura asks Rod about his previous girlfriend. He's brought her up in conversation a couple of times already, and Laura wants to understand why before she goes any further with him.

Rod starts at the beginning.

"We met when I was a ski instructor for a season," he says. "She took lessons and hung around the lodge. She was cute and I was a bit of a player back then, so we started dating almost immediately. As it turned out, she'd just moved to the area and didn't know anyone. We hung out with my friends and I guess our relationship moved pretty quickly—we were living together after a month of dating."

Laura chokes on her droopy fusilli.

"All through that month, she'd been complaining of not feeling great. She kept doing all of these tests and, to be honest, I thought she might be a bit of a hypochondriac. Anyway, about a week after she moved in, we found out that she had cancer. It was scary shit. I didn't know how to help her, and she didn't have any family around. I had to work every day, and so would leave her in the apartment crying and talking to her parents on the phone.

"Her doctor prescribed this one drug for a couple of months. It didn't do anything but make her vomit. The whole apartment smelled of her puke. It was awful. Finally, they figured out that they'd misdiagnosed her."

Laura's fusilli is forgotten. This is a horrible story. No wonder he's still talking about this woman.

"The cancer spread really quickly. It went like wildfire through her body and she was told she'd have to have a double mastectomy."

Laura is near tears.

"I was pretty fed up with the whole thing, but how could I

break up with her when she didn't know anybody and she was going to lose her breasts? I couldn't do it. But we weren't having sex. We weren't laughing any more. We weren't doing anything other than talking about her cancer, her treatment, her breasts, her medication. Her, her, her. It was exhausting.

"She got the mastectomies. That was bad. I thought that maybe she'd feel better once that was done, but she was so depressed. And I couldn't really handle the sight of her naked any more. I know that's terrible to say, but I didn't sign on for a flat-chested woman."

Laura is unaware that her jaw has dropped and that she's clutching her knife.

"After six months, I dumped her. I couldn't deal. I wasn't attracted to her, and she was still crying all the time.

"A year later, she got a $12 million settlement because of the doctor's screw-up. And, get this: When I sent her a letter saying that I think I should get half of the cash, she called me up and told me to go to hell. Can you believe that? I put up with her fucking whining and crying and puking and losing her tits and everything, and she won't give me my fair share of the cash.

He was a jackass for a living

"Anyway, it's kind of preoccupying me now 'cause I'm trying to find a good lawyer so I can sue for the $6 million she owes me. I've got to do it before she spends the whole thing, ha ha."

Bile and the nasty pasta dinner are rising in Laura's chest. She stands on wobbly legs and heads toward the door. She grabs her things and walks out into the night.

✻

IT'S THE FRIDAY NIGHT BEFORE HALLOWEEN. Tasha and Sara, best friends from university, haven't seen each other in ages because of work. They decide to have a couple of pints at Tasha's local.

Catching up with one another is always fun—they are wild women who tell outrageous stories and always have a hoot whenever they're together. So when they catch sight of the table next to them, they're in top form.

"Nice costumes, guys," Tasha says to the four men dressed as Catholic priests. Two of the revellers are older—in their fifties or so—and the other two are stupendously hot young guys in their twenties. Tasha and Sara are both thirty-one and love nothing better than younger men.

"No, really," says the dark-haired young man closest to their table. "We're priests."

"You two, maybe," slurs Sara, pointing to the alarmed older men. "But you? No way, you're too hot."

The second man—rust-coloured curls and blue eyes—pulls some identification from his wallet. Reverend Michael McMillan. It's a valid driver's licence. Holy Mother of. . . .

The dark-haired man leans over to hand Tasha his ID. Reverend Matthew McMillan. Wait a sec.

"Brothers?" she asks. "No way. This is like some nasty Catholic girl's dream."

At this, the two older men remove themselves from the table, raising stern eyebrows at the brothers. "We've got an early morning tomorrow," they say. "Don't stay out too late."

Michael, it turns out, works in a city several hours away, and Matthew ministers to a small town four hours north of the city. They're in town for a seminar.

Tasha is conflicted—she went from feeling lecherous and lusty a minute ago to revering the young men. Having always idealized the Church in some ways, Tasha also has no faith. As Sara gloms on to Michael, Tasha tries to engage Matthew in a conversation about her existential angst. He orders another pint.

Ten minutes later, Sara announces that as hosts of this fair city, they are going to take these Fathers out to a good dance club.

The brothers perk up and insist on changing out of their garb first. They're staying at the university nearby.

As the foursome walk to the priests' rooms, Tasha is trying hard not to think about how attractive Matthew is. *This is my anti-fantasy,* she mutters to herself. *I want to believe in their goodness because I want that for myself.*

At the club, the brothers throw themselves onto the dance floor, dragging Tasha and Sara with them. Taking occasional breaks to catch their breath, the priests buy Tasha and Sara green martinis. The brothers do tequila shots as Sara screams, "Right on, Father! All right!"

A slow song comes on and Matthew pulls Tasha to the dance floor. He moves in close and nuzzles his nose behind her ear to smell her perfume.

"Do you know where I can get some crystal meth?" he asks in a sultry voice.

"Holy fuck, Father," she replies.

When they return to the bar, Sara is waiting for them. She's going to go—she's much too drunk, she explains—and she's already put Michael in a cab back to the university. Matthew asks Tasha to walk him home.

Once outside, he yanks Tasha into a dark alley and starts kissing her. *This is nasty,* she thinks. *But it feels good. Am I going to hell?*

Back at the university dorm, Michael is passed out in bed. Matthew, hands on Tasha's breasts, directs her into the attached bathroom. "It's been five years since I've had sex." He rips off her top. "I want you. Now."

Tasha is overwhelmed by his raw demand. She's also incredibly turned on. Matthew throws off his clothes and devours her.

He flips her into different positions and repeats raunchy porn talk. They have sex without a condom. The only thing that flits across Tasha's hazy mind is that since Matthew's a priest, he must be clean.

It's speedy sex. Matthew is urgent, like a starving man faced with an all-you-can-eat buffet. They collapse on the cold tile floor.

A week later, Tasha e-mails Matthew and asks him to meet her. She wants to resolve her issues of faith and goodness. No reply. She e-mails again, suggesting that she come to his town and they talk about what happened. Again, no reply. She tries to contact him through Michael. No answer.

Has one night with her led him astray? Did she set Matthew, bound by the chains of addiction—to sex, to crystal meth, to her—stumbling down the road to hell? Is she the devil? Or is he too busy hailing Mary, begging for forgiveness? Why has he forsaken her?

Her horny priest, it appears, has disappeared from the face of the earth. Tasha never hears from him. She is, however, thinking of becoming a Buddhist.

Many men complain that women have an appalling tendency to relax too much after marriage, that they let themselves go, bring their beauty gadgets out in the open, and forget their manners.

ARLENE DAHL, *Always Ask a Man: The Key to Femininity*, 1965

Happily Ever After

"I HOPE ALL YOU WANT IS A PLAIN GOLD BAND."

This is how my father proposed to my mother on a warm May evening in 1965.

"Oh. Yeah. That'll be fine," my mother replied, her heart sinking as they walked along the banks of the Ottawa River. She wanted a big ring, a glittering diamond on her finger. But she also knew he was proposing against his will. Sort of.

My father didn't want to get married. It was the era of free love and, at twenty-four, he was too young to settle down. He was never one for much of a fuss. He just wanted to live together. Mum, twenty-one, wasn't keen on that idea. Her values were rather more old-fashioned.

When he was awarded a scholarship for one year of study at the London School of Economics, my father realized that he didn't want to go alone. He'd dated my mother for three years already and loved her very much.

So Dad caved.

Besides, they were compatible. Both had lost fathers while still young children. Both were the middle child of three, raised by strong, independent women. Both were ambitious and excelled in school. And both had big dreams.

One of my mother's big dreams was to have a white wedding in a flower-filled Presbyterian church. She wanted an elegant reception at which guests were served mouth-watering food while music and laughter tinkled in the air. A party at which the wineglasses were always full.

Unfortunately, both were also just out of school and settling into their first serious jobs. My parents had no money.

They set The Date: September 11, 1965. In Vancouver, where their families lived.

By the time the wedding date rolled around, my mother hadn't had any fun planning the big day. My father, still grumpy about bending to societal pressures, had restricted the guest list to twenty people. His mother, who was from an enormous farming family, had sent invitations to forty, all of whom had accepted.

My mother's mother, a grand dame with no cash but plenty of pride, refused to let Mum enjoy a shower (too vulgar) and wouldn't let her register for gifts (entirely too common). She did, however, offer to make a three-tiered fruit cake and have it iced at a local Chinese bakery.

My mother paid for everything. She bought the bridesmaid dress and her mother's dress, and had her wedding dress made by the wife of the janitor at the German embassy. She arranged for her aunt and uncle to host the reception and ordered cream-coloured (to match her parchment-white dress) long-stemmed roses for her bouquet. The minister, upon hearing that Mum was still at a loss for wedding music, offered up his accomplished daughter as the organist. She booked Mr. Whitefoot for photographs—he was the photographer of choice for all of the sororities at the University of British Columbia, and Mum loved how he airbrushed faces.

Dad arranged to borrow his friend's '63 Pontiac convertible for the drive to the church.

One of Dad's many uncles insisted that they use the dusty Cameron family pew bows he'd had at his wedding thirty years earlier. Uncle Lloyd, who lived in Calgary, promised to deliver them on the day of the wedding.

Finally, The Date arrived.

The wedding day started off poorly when my grandmother went off to pick up the cake and discovered that the Chinese baker—never having iced a WASP wedding cake before—had forgotten to use marzipan under the royal icing, and so the decoration was cracking off in large chunks.

The minister called to inform my mother that since this was the first service of the term, the church needed to be cleaned.

"It's full of pigeon feathers and excrement," he said. "You need to vacuum it before people arrive."

"But I have a hair appointment," she said.

"Cancel it."

Mum cancelled her hair appointment and lugged a vacuum over to clean the church. While her fiancé dithered at home, her mother tried to repair the crumbling cake, her brother picked up the flowers, and her bridesmaid preened back at the apartment, Mum scrubbed guano from pews. She wondered where Uncle Lloyd was with those bows.

Uncle Lloyd, as it turned out, was racing across western Canada like a madman to make it to the church on time. He arrived just after Mum finished cleaning.

When she returned to the apartment, she opened the box of flowers to find bright orange roses. She was floored by fatigue and disappointment. As she dressed in a rush, her brother Jim disappeared to find some cream-coloured flowers as a makeshift bouquet.

The actual ceremony passed in a blur. The "organist" was a fifteen-year-old girl who had barely passed her grade eight Royal Conservatory exam, and her playing had everyone clutching their ears. Uncle Lloyd, fried from his maniacal driving, had taken a couple of tranquilizers and couldn't stop plucking at his trousers because, groggy and disoriented, he'd put his underpants on backwards. The Pontiac, when they tried to leave the church, wouldn't start.

At the reception, Mum's mother took a shine to Mr. Whitefoot, the photographer. After ten or so "warm-up" shots, my grandmother interrupted.

"Never mind that, Mr. Whitefoot. You must be parched. Can I get you a drink?" Within an hour, Mr. Whitefoot was stumbling into the furniture and attempting to carve the ham. There are a total of fifteen photographs of my parents' wedding.

During the speeches, Mum's uncle talked about her father, causing Gram to burst into great, heaving sobs. A cousin, desperate to lighten the mood, told the family a dirty joke about the Duchess of Norfolk while Mum suffered a silent death in the corner.

"The Duchess of Norfolk was hiring a new footman," began the cousin. "And she rejected several men before a young local walked in. 'The man I hire will be in my service,' said the duchess. 'And I will require him to be strong, able to carry heavy silver trays and loads of firewood. Roll up your sleeves, young man, and show me your biceps.' The fellow did as she asked and the duchess nodded her approval. 'My footman will wear knee breeches and stockings and so he must have firm, nice calves. Roll up your pants and show me your calves.' Again, the young man did as she asked. 'You have a fine calf, my young man,' said the duchess. 'Now I'm going to have to see your testimonials.'

"Later that night, the young man was sharing a pint with his friend. 'If I'd had a better education,' he sighed, 'I would've got that job.'"

Mum's family peed themselves laughing. Dad's family was a sea of blank faces. They didn't understand the joke.

They did, however, get uproariously drunk. This is how Dad's mother, a teetotaller, found out that her siblings were heavy boozers.

And Uncle Lloyd collapsed.

He'd been drinking heavily. He had a history of heart trouble. Halfway through the reception, he sank to the floor. Terrible luck for a bride and groom, Mum and Dad were hustled out of their own reception. In the sputtering 1963 Pontiac, my parents went to the White Spot (a greasy spoon) to eat their wedding meal—hamburgers—and wait to hear if Dad's uncle had died.

Once he drank some water and turned his underpants around, Uncle Lloyd felt much better, and even managed to down three more flutes of champagne at the reception.

IN SEPTEMBER 2005, my parents will celebrate their fortieth wedding anniversary. Their bad date—the ultimate bad date—might never have happened had they not both been madly in love. At any point during that proposal, engagement, wedding, and reception, my mother or father might have blamed kismet and thrown in the towel. (My mother is quick to add, "But look at the husband I have now. He's wonderful. If I hadn't put up with all of that, I wouldn't be with him.")

Couples do go through terrible, embarrassing, and cringe-worthy moments together. The most awful of these situations tends to happen when a couple is dating, when there's no ring to bind them together for better or for worse. And then the worst that happens is that they break up. In the best of circumstances, however, these events serve to make a relationship stronger (and provide fodder to entertain their children down the road).

The following stories are from couples that, despite the odds, remain together. They all share a common element: Despite inauspicious beginnings, they found the fairy-tale ending. They pulled the pink ribbon from that gorgeous cream-coloured box and realized their dreams.

*

"MUFFIN TINS? Anybody have muffin tins?"

"I do!" I scream. "Bingo! Bingo! I win!" I hoot and high-five my friend Kat, who's sitting next to me. By the ensuing silence, I reckon I'm a little too loud and enthusiastic for this particular wedding shower and settle down.

We're playing Bridal Bingo. If you've never had the pleasure, here's how it works. A card is organized in the same way as the traditional game but, rather than numbers, it's filled with the names of potential shower gifts. As the bride-to-be opens each new gift, guests check their cards and, if they have it, cross the item off. Mark a whole row of, say, "something blue," "wineglasses," "oh so naughty," "frying pan," and "muffin tins" and the lucky guest wins a prize.

I win a bag full of beauty products from the Body Shop. Excellent. I'm hoping there will be some lip balm. My lips are so dry; they bled when I shouted bingo. Aha! There it is. Ahhhh, soothing balm. Bless the Body Shop.

It's only later, once I'm home and going through my loot, that I see the words *labial cream* printed on the lip balm. What? Labial cream? Surely it's not for my, uh, other lips?

I'm trying to figure out how this balm should be used by sniffing it, when my boyfriend calls.

"Hey babe," he says. "What's up?"

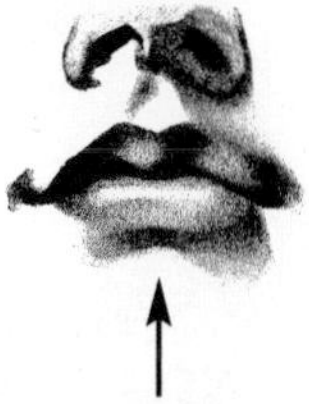

I explain what I'm doing. "It doesn't smell sexy. . . ."

"I think it's for your face lips," says John patiently. "I can't imagine Annette putting cootch cream in the grab bags." I have to agree that it's unlikely my prim hostess would've felt so liberated.

Labia?

Over the next few months, every time I use the balm in John's presence, we crack jokes about my labial cream and its many uses.

Cut to Thanksgiving. We're off to my parents' house for dinner. It's the first holiday that John has spent with my family and it's a big deal. The final stamp of approval will occur if Dad lets him carve the turkey. Walking in, we see that my sister, her boyfriend, our minister, and his wife have arrived. It's a rowdy crowd. Really. Add a few glasses of wine and no one can get a word in edgewise.

Before dinner, we're all in the kitchen "helping" my mother with the turkey (that means whenever her back is turned we're picking off the crispy strips of bacon that she's cooked on top of it) and I'm rummaging through the fridge trying to find the cranberry sauce. John and my sister are chatting. Our minister is joking with my sister's boyfriend and Dad is squeezing lotion onto his perpetually dry hands.

"I don't know why," my father says to no one in particular, "but my lips are so dry this fall." He rubs some lotion across his mouth.

"That's interesting, David," John pipes up. "Amy has a similar problem. Why don't you try some of her labial cream?"

The room falls silent. From the depths of the fridge, I screech, "*John!*"

Labia cream rocks!

All eyes turn to me and I blush crimson.

"Oh. I thought you'd told your dad," says John, a sly smile on his face. "Sorry."

Dad carved the bird.

SATURDAY MORNING, 11:20 A.M.

"Emily? I'm going outside for a smoke."

"Okay. I'll join you in a sec."

My cheeks burning, I engage in a quick sniff test. Could Tom smell that? I have, for maybe the twelfth time in our two-year relationship, ducked into Tom's bathroom to poo. Normally, I'd wait until I got home (I come from a long line of anal women, excuse the reference, who refuse to acknowledge the fact that they have colons and therefore always have an animal in the house to blame for any errant farts). Unfortunately, this morning, an urgent rumbling after a bacon and eggs breakfast sent me scurrying to the washroom.

When such a situation arises, I insist on setting a time limit—I never allow myself more time in the bathroom than it would take to pee. In case there is a decidedly number two–ishness about the bathroom when I'm done, I have developed a series of arm movements designed to air out the room at top speed. Should that fail, at least Tom can marvel at my efficiency. But this morning, when the urge struck, Tom was on the phone. I decided to risk it.

In fact, I even relaxed. I thought he'd be chatting for a while and so lost track of time. Absorbed in a magazine article called "Storage Solutions for Every Home," I was startled when Tom actually came to the bathroom door to inform me of his whereabouts. Yikes. Gotta get out of here now. Time's up.

Flush. I turn to the tap and start to wash my hands. Out of the corner of my eye, I notice that instead of draining, the toilet is filling. Filling up. The drain is clogged. Oh. My. God.

I try flushing it again. And, again, the water rises, but this time it comes dangerously close to the edge of the bowl. Fuck. Shit. No! No shit—I want to get rid of the shit. Tom's waiting. He's going to think I'm constipated. I don't even want him to know that I poo. I'm human, of course, but I don't want to be *that* human. Where's the plunger?

Scanning the bathroom I realize, in slow-motion terror, that *there is no plunger.*

I'll just reach in, then. I'll just grab the poo and toss it . . . where? Out the window. I'll toss it out the window. That's no problem. Oh, except for the downstairs neighbour who's digging out weeds. Well, I could toss it and then duck out of sight before she sees me. How will she know that the poo is coming from this apartment? When she comes to the door, I'll just look at her in scorn and say, "Poo coming from the sky? Maybe the shit just hit the fan." Then she'll leave, embarrassed to have interrupted our morning with such nonsense, and quietly bury my poo in her garden.

"Em?" calls Toms. "You coming?"

"Yup!" I force myself to respond with a cheery falsetto that no self-respecting woman currently contemplating throwing her own poo out the window of her boyfriend's bathroom would ever feel. "Be right there." No time.

I close the lid and decide to deal with it after I've clubbed Tom over the head "accidentally" so that he has to lie down and I thereby gain at least twenty minutes to do some poo tossing.

"You all right?" Tom asks as I join him on the front porch with my cup of tea. "You look pale."

"Fine," I say, kissing him on the cheek. "I got caught up in an article about storage solutions. I'm thinking I should build a rolling bookshelf that can hide another underneath it. What do you think? Or I could hang suitcases from the ceiling for knick-knacks and other junk."

Tom stares at me for a moment and then gamely starts weighing the pros and cons of bedskirts versus pretty baskets for the mess under my bed.

I remember that I'm supposed to knock him out. I'm inching my arm toward the shovel leaning against the side of the porch when he says, "I'm just going to use the washroom."

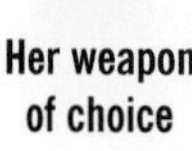

Her weapon of choice

"NO!"

"What?" Tom says. "Why not?"

"Because . . . because, well, I'd rather not say," I answer. "It's a secret."

"Emily, are you okay?"

"Fine. No problem. I'm just working on something in there and I don't want you to see it."

"Is it a gift?" Tom starts to smile. "You've made me a gift of your poo and you're not done yet?"

Holy Mother of God. This is awful. If only I had the skill of projectile vomiting at will, I could avoid where this conversation is headed. I try to gag.

"Emily," Tom says. "What's going on? Are you . . . gagging?"

"Uh, it's just that. . . ." Oh, God, please help me in my time of need. A power outage. A wild boar. Anything. "I seem to have—that is, the toilet appears to be, um, well, blocked."

"Shit."

"Yes. Well, toilet paper mostly." My eyes fill with tears. It's possible I may actually vomit spontaneously.

Tom looks at me and starts to giggle. This is not funny. This is not amusing. This is when my fury kicks in.

"Why don't you have a plunger? Any man worth his salt has

a plunger located directly beside the toilet so his girlfriend can avoid this exact situation! This is, really, your fault. It's a necessity. Every household should have a plunger."

"I've never needed one before."

I could kill him. In fact, I might kill him. I start to reach for the shovel again, but then he says, "You're right, but shit happens. C'mon let's go buy a plunger."

Walking home with our new $8 plunger, we bump into every person we know. There's no way to hide a plunger. It's right there. But most people just look at us with sympathy and don't ask. When this happens, I grimace and roll my eyes toward Tom.

Upon returning to the scene, Tom offers to plunge but I grab the tool from his grasp and say goodbye to my beloved. "If this doesn't work," I say, "we're breaking up."

"No way. I'm not going along with that."

"I'm sorry, but that's just the way it has to be. If this doesn't work *and* the toilet overflows, I'm going to leave by the back door and move to Tahiti. We'll never talk again. I love you. Goodbye."

Tom kisses me.

Five minutes later, I return the conquering hero and announce that our relationship can continue. There is much rejoicing, but I'll be damned if I ever poo there again.

"HI, SUE."

"Kalie. How are you?"

"Okay, now. But for a while I thought the marriage was off."

"What!?"

"I brought Benoit to meet the parental unit a couple of nights ago."

"Didn't they like your fabulous fiancé?"

"Well, he didn't say a word at first. It didn't help that when we got there my parents were in the middle of a long conversation with my sister in Dutch. He can't understand a word.

"Then they asked him very direct questions. It was okay, I guess. They asked him about being French and his family and all of that. He eventually got more comfortable and it was nice. They asked about the wedding plans and he remembered not to talk about the guest list."

"Sounds good."

"Remember that Dutch phrase I taught you when we lived together?"

"*Noiken* in the *koiken?* How could I forget? I love that expression."

"Benoit knows it too, now. And whenever we're necking in the kitchen, he's like, 'Hey, we're *neuken* in the *keuken.*' He says it all Anglo, like you.

"Anyway, Benoit and I were in the kitchen after dinner, washing dishes. He was kissing the back of my neck, his arms wrapped around me, when Mom came in. She saw us and said in a jokey, angry way: 'Hey. What's going on in here?' Benoit pipes up, 'We're *noiken* in the *koiken.*' Mom's face froze. In a very real, very angry way, she says to Benoit, 'We don't say those words in this house, Benoit.' She turns and walks out."

"What? Why?"

"I didn't understand it, but she was so pissed—all red in the face—that I didn't bring it up again. We finished the dishes, said thank you, and got the hell out of there. I talked to her about it yesterday and she barely let me get a word in edgewise. 'Kalie, you cannot marry a man who speaks like that.' 'So disrespectful.' 'What must his family be like?'

"I told her that I'd taught him that expression. Then she was furious with me. 'Of all the Dutch words, why would you teach him that filth? What's wrong with you? Is he going to say it at the wedding? To my family?' She was screeching. I was, like, 'Mom, calm down. It just means necking in the kitchen.'"

"What did she say?"

"She started to laugh. Apparently, the combination of Benoit's accent and my bad Dutch came out as 'fucking the chicken.'"

"What?"

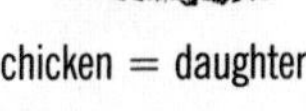
chicken = daughter

"Yeah. My fiancé meets my parents for the first time and I've taught him to say, 'Oh, yeah, just fucking the chicken here.' The chicken, of course, being their daughter."

Before the wedding, Kalie's mother made Benoit promise not to use any Dutch words. He obliged.

*

REBECCA IS A VOLUPTUOUS REDHEAD. When she enters a room, men drop drinks on the floor. On the night in question, she'd been single for four months—a long stretch in her world but after a disastrous love affair, she'd sworn off men forever. In fact, she didn't even want to go out that evening but her girlfriends had persuaded her with promises of silly conversations about nothing remotely serious. After a long week spent dealing with the anal-retentive owner of a restaurant she was decorating, she needed some fun, so Rebecca agreed to join her friends for drinks at a pool hall after work.

She noticed Lindsay almost immediately. Still in school, he was out with some friends celebrating the end of exams. In a fortunate twist of fate, one of his friends knew one of her friends. The groups merged to play a round of pool.

"Hi." Lindsay walked over to Rebecca, who was perched on a barstool. "I'm Lindsay."

"Lindsay?"

"Yeah."

"I hate that name. I'm sorry, but I do. A friend of mine is married to a Lindsay who's a real jerk. I can't stand him and now I associate the name with assholes." As soon as the words were out of her mouth, Rebecca regretted them. She was horrified with herself.

You display the wonderful traits of charm and courtesy.
Far East Fortune Cookie Co. Ltd. (416) 977-2482

What am I doing? A tall, handsome man strikes up a conversation with me and I diss him? I'm obviously not ready to be dating again. And who says he wants to date? Oh, dear, all he said was hello.

"I'm so sorry. I don't know what I'm saying," gushed Rebecca. "I do hate the name, but I shouldn't automatically assume you're an asshole just because your parents named you Lindsay."

I did it again. Someone shoot me.

"Lindsay, I'm sorry. I'm not going to talk any more. That was so rude. I'm Rebecca."

Lindsay, taken aback, recovered quickly.

"Well, Rebecca. Since we're being honest, I've always hated redheads. Until now, I've never found a red-headed woman attractive."

Rebecca and Lindsay were married in the summer of 2002.

*

MARCH 11, 10 P.M.

Whatever happens, I will not sleep with Colin. I will not, no matter how desperately I want to, have sex with Colin. I will be strong. I will be flirtatious and funny and charming and fabulous. But I will not get nasty with Colin.

I'm driving to Beaconsfield tomorrow afternoon for our date. We're having dinner. We're going out for drinks. I will have two, no more. I'm spending the night on his couch. I will not sleep with Colin.

I really want to sleep with Colin.

* * *

March 13, 2:08 a.m.

There's no way I'm sleeping with Colin. Maybe ever. I'm writing this curled up on his lumpy sofa with a tattered blanket for warmth and a pillow so old its better days were back in the 1950s.

Driving down this afternoon, I went through a terrific snowstorm—it was insane. I've never seen hail like that before. Huge, round balls pinging off the windshield, making the most horrible cracking sound. Unbelievable.

I get to town, feeling a little rattled from the long drive, and meet Colin at the tiny French restaurant a block and a half from his place. It's so cozy in there. After being in the car, I felt like I was walking into a warm bath. The restaurant has dark wood walls, heavy burgundy curtains, and plush velvet cushions on the seats. A perfect date location.

He's already there and has a bottle of white wine chilling. It was so sweet, actually. I told him on our first date that I didn't like red wine but loved white and he remembered. Little gestures like that make me swoon. If only men knew how easy it is. . . .

Anyway, as soon as the waiter takes our order, it's like we've been together for years. Like we're made for each other. Granted, we've known each other for five years now, but this is a date. It's different. Only it's not different. We're bursting with things we've wanted to talk about on the phone for the last week but have saved for this date. We talk about the upcoming election and about the shoddy news coverage. We argue over the best candidate in my riding and he tells me about working in Geneva for a year. There's not enough time in the world for us to say everything we want to.

Supper ends up taking so long—we linger over dessert—that we decide to go straight back to his place.

It's the first time I've ever seen where he lives. It's so strange. I can't decide if it's awful or cool. No, I can. It's awful. The apartment is gorgeous—big, spacious, huge windows. But instead of real, adult furniture, he has a forest-green plastic lawn table and chairs in his kitchen. The sofa I'm lying on is plaid. He's got one chair. His desktop is propped up with plastic milk cartons and there are books everywhere: on the table, kitchen counter, living room floor, desk, the one chair, and even his bed.

Before I really take any of this in, though, Colin does something I'll never forget. We walk in and he removes his shoes. He reaches into the hall closet, pulls out a pair of battered leather mules—the kind very old Italian men wear—and slips his feet into them. He then rummages for something else. His arm draws back to reveal a beige cardigan with leather patches on the elbows.

Colin is Mr. Rogers.

But that's not the worst bit.

He gets me a beer—Carlsberg, blech—and we sit, close and comfy, on the couch. He starts talking about his time spent living in Campbellsville, describing the scene he was part of there. There was a large group of close friends who did everything together—camping, partying, vacationing, eating, sleeping. A bit incestuous, a lot of fun. He tells me about Shirley, the girl he dated for a few months there.

"She was odd." Colin shifts position on the couch. "She had a few strange obsessions."

I'm thinking that I don't really want to hear about Shirley strapping booster cables to his nipples or anything. I am so far off base.

"She was a big fan of *Star Trek*."

"You dated a Trekkie?" I howl.

"Yeah. She loved it. Posters and figurines—you name it, she had it."

"I'm amazed you put up with that."

"It wasn't that bad. I mean, I enjoy the show. I'm not about to start dressing up or anything but. . . ."

"What?" I'm intrigued.

"Uh, I guess I did dress up as a member of the *Enterprise*."

I start to giggle.

"It was for Halloween, and Shirley really wanted to go as a couple from the *Enterprise*. She made the costumes and everything. Hold on." He leaps up and races down the hall, his slippers shuffling in double time.

A few minutes pass. I'm just about to get up and investigate when I hear him call. "Promise you won't laugh?"

"Promise." My fingers are crossed.

He shuffles back down the hall. I look up.

Colin is dressed head to toe in a skin-tight beige *Enterprise* costume. When I say skin-tight, I mean he obviously has nothing on underneath and he must have gained weight since he was originally measured for the hideous thing. The slightly shiny polyester material highlights every ripple, bump, dip, curve, and hanging bit. The only thing he's kept on from his previous outfit is the mules.

Mules are the new black.

"I always thought I looked pretty good in this," says the man I always thought of as modest and conservative, as he does a small pirouette. I can't contain myself. Tears stream down my cheeks. I am hysterical. When I eventually pull myself together, I am on the floor clutching my aching belly.

Colin watches me without comment and then turns on his mules and leaves the room.

Note: It would be two very long weeks before Colin called for another date. It took him a while, but he finally saw the humour in the situation (and threw out the costume).

❄

"IT'D BE NICE IF SOMETIMES you opened the door for me or held out my chair," says Kelly.

From the opposite side of the table, Les looks sheepish. For their three-month anniversary, Kelly organized a lovely night. She made reservations at a trendy new fusion restaurant and bought Les a book he'd been wanting to read.

Les, on the other hand, had forgotten that it was supposed to be a special night.

Kelly is a student at the town's university and Les, a local, works for his father. They met through mutual friends and fell in love. They enjoy so many of the same things—beer, hockey, eighties music, and reading—that they're never at a loss for conversation. And the sex is phenomenal. The only problem is that Les is a bit gauche at times.

"I think that chivalry is an important yet lost art among men these days," Kelly continues. When Les showed up *sans* gift, wearing stained, ripped jeans, and sporting two-day stubble growth, Kelly determined it was time to air her concerns. She didn't think she could continue to date a man who was such a . . . *guy*.

"It's a matter of being gracious and polite and thoughtful and—"

"I'll try," interrupts Les. "I know I can be obtuse, and I'm sorry. Chivalry awaits. You deserve nothing less."

Satisfied, Kelly changes the subject. They don't talk about it again.

Later that night, they return—quite looped on rum and Cokes—to the tiny closet that Les calls his bedroom. His bed, a sheet of plywood supported by five-foot wood beams under which a few boxes serve as a makeshift desk, takes up most of the room. Climbing into bed, Les turns on the ancient space heater that provides the only comfort in the small room. The element burns red-hot.

Tonight, it smells suspicious.

"What happens if that space heater catches on fire?" Kelly eyeballs the contraption.

"I'll wake up, kick out the window, and rescue you, my princess," replies Les.

Ten minutes later, he lurches to the side of the bed. "Gotta go. Bathroom," he chokes.

Kelly watches as he stumbles over the space heater. He turns, as though to say something, and vomits all over the floor.

"Kell, I'm afraid chivalry is dead."

As Kelly tells this story, years later, she twists her wedding band around her finger. "Even with spots of puke dotting his face, Les was able to make me laugh," she smiles. "He's still rotten at opening doors, though."

*

A MONTH INTO THE NEW ROMANCE, Mark surprised Christine with a picnic on the Toronto Islands. Using an old wicker basket that belonged to his parents, he packed cold cuts, cheese, grapes, pickles, and cookies. He added two bottles of Wolf Blass yellow label and three condoms. They rode their bikes onto the ferry and canoodled on the deck, under the sun.

They took pictures of each other buried in sand and ate their meal in a mossy glen. They told each other their second-deepest secrets and giggled over the fleshy, pale bodies on the nude beach. They tossed grapes into each other's mouths—Christine hit the tip of Mark's nose, causing him to laugh so hard he farted. They drifted off under an old elm, arms wrapped around each other.

When they awoke, Christine was filled with longing for Mark. She looked at him and raised one eyebrow. A lazy smile crossed his lips and he jerked his head in the direction of the beach. Without uttering a word, they rose and gathered their things. They moved their bikes off the path, hiding them in some bushes.

They were wearing dark enough clothing that no one would be able to see them from the path. Mark, dropping his cut-offs to the sand, sat on a large piece of driftwood and patted his lap. Lifting her skirt, Christine lowered herself onto his rigid penis. A perfect fit. Pure ecstasy.

Tension mounted. Extremities tingled. Birds sang. The sun sank. Just before their world would shatter in a moment of sweet bliss, Mark jumped up, shoving Christine off of him. She landed in the sand and stared up at Mark.

Her boyfriend was scrabbling at his testicles.

"Oh no, oh no, oh no," he repeated, his voice much higher than usual. "Oh, this hurts. It hurts."

He looked at Christine and she saw his eyes filling with tears. "Something's wrong!" he cried.

The panic on his face shot terror through her heart. He placed his hands on his bottom, wiping them up and down. "Help me. Help. It hurts."

Christine leapt to her feet and ran to Mark.

"What can I do?" she asked.

"C-c-can you l-l-look?" he stammered.

"Okay. Yes." She knelt before his penis.

Hampered by the shorts still around his ankles, Mark twisted around. He bent over and pulled his bum cheeks apart. "L-l-look there."

Christine had never looked in someone's bum before. Swallowing nervous laughter, she leaned in for closer examination.

Swarming the sweet pink pucker of Mark's behind was an army of fire ants.

It was at that moment, brushing ants from his bottom, that Christine knew how fiercely she loved this man. She knew—absolutely, wholly, finally—that it must be True Love if she was willing to wipe his ass.

The second thing which you may make sure of is, that however good you may be, you have faults; that however dull you may be, you can find out what some of them are; and that however slight they may be, you had better make some—not too painful, but patient—effort to get quit of them.

JOHN RUSKIN, *Pearls for Young Ladies*, 1878

Pearls of Wisdom

HAVING READ TOO MANY BOOKS brimming with dating advice, I tried to avoid burdening this book with any unwelcome tidbits of wisdom. If one were to seek my counsel, I would refer them to the pearls that fell from my grandmother's mouth—offered with a stiff gin and tonic—that appear in the dedication of this book.

After writing up all of these stories, however, it occurred to me that the best people to offer any pointers on dating would be the men and women who contributed in ways both great and small to this book.

Finally, in their own words, I give you the following advice:

1. Never date a guy who drives a Mustang.
2. Never date a guy that you could beat up.
3. Never date a guy prettier than you.

—ENGAGED WOMAN, AGE THIRTY

Never tell your date, at any point in the evening, that you have renounced your usual practice of hopping into bed on the first night, because then you most assuredly will. If you are a bad girl—and, let's face it, you most probably are—nothing turns your crank more than being rebellious. But once you've declared that you're not going to do something naughty, you will rebel against that fake sanctimony and do the dirty deed.

Don't even think about *not* going to bed on a first date. If the chemistry's there, you will. If it isn't, you won't be tempted.

—WOMAN IN HER SECOND MARRIAGE, AGE FIFTY

1. Always be direct with people. Nothing facilitates ease between people more than truth. If your truths don't match, both parties can move on without injury.
2. Never sleep with someone on the first date. When you give it up right out of the gate, all sorts of emotions are stirred up and it messes with one's ability to process information about a prospective partner in a rational manner. At least, that's what I hear.

—SINGLE MAN, AGE THIRTY-SIX

Always have an out—go for drinks, not dinner.

—SINGLE WOMAN, AGE THIRTY-FIVE

Never spit half-chewed soda crackers at girls in an attempt to mimic a cat dry-heaving and impress them with your chameleon-like abilities. You *will* be thrown out of whatever establishment you are in, and you *will* get slapped.

—DIVORCED MALE, AGE THIRTY-EIGHT

Don't date your cousin.

—MARRIED WOMAN, AGE FORTY-SEVEN

Try to remember your date's name.

—SINGLE MALE, AGE THIRTY-THREE

Good shoes on a man is the first indication that he is a man worth dating.

—ENGAGED WOMAN, AGE THIRTY-TWO

1. Don't change who you are for anyone. If there is anything you're concerned about, don't ignore your instincts. Any problem will only magnify and become worse once you are living together or married.
2. Make your mate/husband your best friend and communicate about everything.
3. Always feel comfortable when walking around your bedroom naked.

—MARRIED WOMAN, AGE THIRTY

1. Approach dating as you would a job interview. It's about seeing if there is a fit, so *never* feel bad if there isn't one. Enjoy the evening, or take notes so you can reflect on your adventures in dating when you are good and married.
2. Expand your horizons. Kiss a lot of toads before you meet your prince.

—MARRIED WOMAN, AGE THIRTY-FIVE

Never try to show off while bowling on your first date.

—JUST-MARRIED WOMAN, AGE THIRTY-THREE

❋

MY PERSONAL FAVOURITE comes from the oldest contributor to the book:

> What the heck. Life is lots of fun. When in doubt, risk it!
>
> —WOMAN, MARRIED FORTY-SEVEN YEARS, AGE SEVENTY-ONE

Acknowledgements

IMAGINE CHECKING YOUR E-MAIL one afternoon and finding a request for your most embarrassing and funniest date story. It will be published, for thousands to read, and you've just got to trust this Amy Cameron person to keep your details safe. It takes a confident woman to hit reply and spill the beans but so many people did. I will be forever indebted to every single one of them. The generosity and humour of women from around the world is humbling. This book would not exist without you. Thank you so very much.

Whether they like it or not, I will name two among those wonderful contributors. Kathryn Borel was my Reader and secret weapon at the Bad Date parties and Paulette Goguen told me the horrible, hilarious date that started it all. Both went above and beyond the call of duty.

When I was seventeen years old, Neil McDonald took me out and showed me a terrible time. It was a bad date that turned into a lifelong friendship. *Playing With Matches* was his idea–hatched over a latte after I shared Paulette's story with him–and for that, I can't thank Neil enough.

It's no secret that there is an amazing team of women at Doubleday Canada. Martha Kanya-Forstner, my editor, worked like a dog, kept giggling, and made the manuscript a better read. The lovely yet twisted touch of art director Kelly Hill had me laughing out loud. And I would be remiss if I didn't also heap praise upon Amy Black, Jennifer Shepherd, and Sharon Klein for their commitment to this project.

Walking in to the offices of Westwood Creative Artists was the second best idea I ever had. Linda McKnight, my patient and fabulous agent, is a dream.

Writing a book does not always highlight one's best features. My roommate, Jim Donald, fed cats without complaint and weathered evenings filled with women moaning that there are "no good single men left" (there are, ladies–one was hiding upstairs). Bill and Janet Rowley provided me with a safe haven, complete with distracting entertainment and delicious meals.

Without the endless love and support from my family, I'd be curled up in a ball somewhere. I am so blessed. Tassie Cameron's sharp wit and eye for detail helped form the tone of this book. The research, pacing, and shape of stories, I learned at the feet of a master—Stevie Cameron. David Cameron encouraged me to take risks and caught me every time I fell.

The best idea I ever had was to date John Rowley. His love, honesty, and humour keep me grounded. He also came up with what I still think might be the best title for this book. Ours has never been a relationshit.

Sources

Antelle,Yvonne, *How to Catch and Hold a Man,* New York: Essandess Special Editions, 1967.

Arlene Dahl, *Always Ask A Man,* Englewood Cliffs, NJ, Prentice-Hall,1965.

Hirsch, Edwin W., *The Power to Love,* New York: Citadel Press, 1934.

Morgan, Marabel, *The Total Woman,* New York: Fleming H. Revell Co., 1973.

Emily Post, *Etiquette,* New York: HarperResource, 2004.

About the Author

AMY CAMERON is an award-winning journalist. Her work has appeared in *Maclean's* magazine and the *New Brunswick Telegraph-Journal.* She currently lives, and dates, in Toronto. *Playing with Matches: Misadventures in Dating* is her first book.

To read more dating nightmares, please visit
www.misadventuresindating.com